T0038321

TREE SPIRITS GRASS SPIRITS

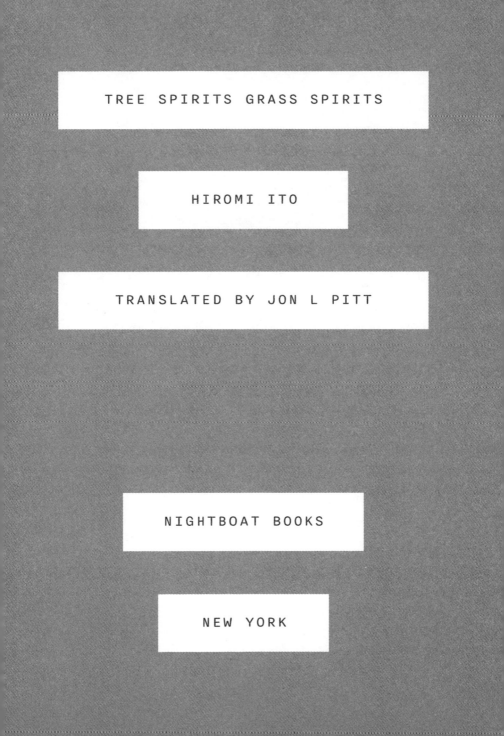

TREE SPIRITS GRASS SPIRITS

HIROMI ITO

TRANSLATED BY JON L PITT

NIGHTBOAT BOOKS

NEW YORK

ISBN: 978-1-64362-192-0

Cover art: Front: tumbleweed; back: mountain lilac, both 2014
© Becky Cohen
Courtesy of the artist
Design and typesetting by Kit Schluter
Typeset in Adobe Caslon Pro and Nitti Typewriter

Cataloging-in-publication data is available from the Library of Congress

Nightboat Books
New York
www.nightboat.org

CONTENTS

TRANSLATOR'S PREFACE

Tree Spirits Grass Spirits is a collection of Hiromi Ito's seemingly stand-alone meditations on plant life, published serially between April 2012 and November 2013 by Iwanami Shoten in their monthly periodical *Tosho*. Iwanami Shoten is known mostly as a publisher of academic books, and one gets the sense that Ito approached these pieces with a somewhat scholarly audience in mind. Indeed, for readers familiar with Hiromi Ito's previously published translations, which include the poetry collection *Killing Kanoko* and the long-form narrative poem *Wild Grass on the Riverbank* (both translated by Jeffrey Angles), this present book may look surprisingly quotidian and conventional. To be sure, there remains a playfulness and experimental ethos at work in *Tree Spirits Grass Spirits*, but by and large it does not feature many of the qualities readers likely associate with Ito's previously published translations. Formally, it appears more like prose than poetry, to a degree even higher than *The Thorn Puller* (also translated by Angles), which is ostensibly a "novel" but is composed largely of poetic language that draws from centuries of Japanese poetic tradition. And where *Killing Kanoko* and *Wild Grass on the Riverbank* revel in the grotesqueries of sex and death, *Tree Spirits Grass Spirits* presents a more subtle take on these topics—less shocking, perhaps, but no less profound or poetic.

In June of 2022, I shared the stage with Ito and her Norwegian translator, Ika Kaminka, at a reading event at the University of Oslo.

I read from a work-in-progress version of this book, Ika read from her work-in-progress Norwegian translation of *The Thorn Puller*, and Ito read from the original Japanese. During our conversation on stage, I asked Ito if she herself thought of these two books— *Tree Spirits Grass Spirits* and *The Thorn Puller*—as works of poetry despite their prose-like appearances. She responded that as time goes by, she thinks of them more and more as a kind of poetry. We discussed why she does not consider the chapters of *Tree Spirits Grass Spirits* "essays"—a term she has been actively pushing against in the past few years. For Ito, essays are trivial, commonplace things. She then turned the question around on me: did I, as the translator, think of *Tree Spirits Grass Spirits* as poetry, or as a collection of essays? I responded that I think of it as a work of philosophy.

I stand by this claim. *Tree Spirits Grass Spirits* is a work of philosophy, albeit a subtle and poetic one that develops slowly—much like a plant. While each chapter can be read and appreciated on its own, new things will undoubtedly appear when reading the chapters alongside one another—much like a garden. Many of the book's central concerns—ontological and epistemological knowledge of plant life, travel, motherhood, immigration, and death— are treated with a metaphysical seriousness that sneaks up on the reader. Profound images and lyric passages reverberate between chapters. Indeed, the word "tree spirits" or "*kodama*" found in the book's title can also mean "echoes." A philosophy of plant life and its relationship to our own human lives echoes in the background of each chapter as Ito navigates between moments of repetition and more straightforward narrative passages that read like travelogue or memoir.

Ultimately, it is difficult to categorize *Tree Spirits Grass Spirits* as any particular genre. This ambiguity is fitting. It mirrors the difficultly in classifying plant life that serves as a central focus of the book itself. Translating a book about plants presents a unique challenge, as one plant can have many names. There are common names, which may vary by region. There are scientific names, but these categorizations may change over time. Entire plant families are incorporated into other families, and their names along with them. In short, the naming and classifying of plant life is far from stable and remains highly contextual to a given place and time. This fact becomes all the more apparent when translating a work like *Tree Spirits Grass Spirits*—a book not just about plants, but also very much about how we name and classify, and thus come to understand, plants. It is a book about language as much as it is about plant life. And it is, in turn, very much about how we understand our all-too-human senses of time and place in reference to plant life. For Ito, who writes this book from the perspective of a Japanese woman who has immigrated to the United States, the somewhat arbitrary status of plant life as either native, naturalized, or invasive to a given place becomes a framework to rethink one's own position in a new land. Thus we find her lamenting the removal of "invasive" ice plant in Southern California, identifying with the "naturalized" oxalis that her gardener calls a "weed," and questioning the categorization of cucumber grass in Japan as "naturalized" instead of "native," despite its long history on the Japanese archipelago. She asks of the cucumber grass: "If it were humans we were talking about, wouldn't they already be considered fellow countrymen? As a humble immigrant myself, this is a question I can't let go of."

Much of *Tree Spirits Grass Spirits* takes place outside of Japan. Ito was living in Southern California at the time of its writing, but, as the book makes clear, she frequently was traveling between the US, Japan, and Europe. As a record of this transnational travel, the book is, in many ways, already a work of translation. Ito writes often about plants not found in Japan, but for a Japanese audience. And when she *does* write about plants a Japanese readership would know, she regularly invites them to see these in a new environment, be it

the dry wasteland of Southern California or the snowy streets of
Berlin. This means that, at any given time, Ito may use one or more
of the following names for a plant: 1) its Japanese common name,
2) its Japanese scientific name, 3) its Latin scientific name, or 4)
its common English name. Add to these the names that Ito makes
up in Japanese, whole cloth, when she doesn't know any of the
above name-types (as she writes about in the chapter "Eucalyptus
Tobacco Party"), and the proliferation is abundant. But all of these
names carry different weight and meaning, and they are carefully
chosen by the author. In short, it matters to the story (and to the
poetry) which name Ito uses in a particular moment.

In his excellent translation of *Wild Grass on the Riverbank*, Jeffrey
Angles renders the majority of the plant names in Latinized sci-
entific terminology. Here are Ito's thoughts on this decision, taken
from the chapter "*Arexa kawaransis*" of this book: "In the English
translation (of *Wild Grass on the Riverbank*), the plant names be-
came Latinized. The English names for plants bear traces of peo-
ple's everyday lives and emotions, like horseweed (which is the
English name for *himemukashiyomogi*) or Johnson grass (which is
the English name for *seibanmorokoshi*). They are the everyday lives
and emotions of strangers, and so I feel no empathy for them." In
Wild Grass on the Riverbank, the Latinization of plant names works
beautifully to emphasize the defamiliarization of plant names and
create a poetic aura that resembles the chanting of mantras (as Ito
describers in the opening chapter of this book). But I discovered
early on that this approach would not work for *Tree Spirits Grass
Spirits*, as this book is specifically about the disconnect Ito points
to in the quote above—namely, that different names bear differ-
ent traces of "everyday lives and emotions." Because this is a book
about everyday lives and emotions, I needed to keep them in the
translation.

I decided I would need to take each mention of plants on a case-by-case basis. When Ito specifically uses the Latinized scientific name, I have followed suit. When she uses the common English name, I again have followed suit. Things get trickier with the Japanese scientific and common names. For the most part, I have tried to avoid simply rendering these into their English counterparts. So, for example, when Ito writes of *seitaka-awadachisō*, I tend to leave it transliterated (as I do in the chapter titled "Traveling with *Seitaka-awadachisō*"), although I do offer a parenthetical with the English name from time to time in order to allow the English reader a chance to look it up themselves. My thinking is this: when Ito is writing about *seitaka-awadachisō*, she is writing about the plant from its Japanese perspective, full of the "everyday life and emotion" of someone who has lived alongside it on the riverbanks of Southern Japan. When she travels to Michigan and finds the plant on the roadside (as she does in the previously mentioned chapter), Ito is not thinking or writing about "Canadian goldenrod" (which is the English common name for the plant). She is ruminating on the plant that has naturalized to Japan, i.e., *seitaka-awadachisō*, and how it may differ from the native version found in North America, i.e., goldenrod. Because of this case-by-case method, this book features more transliterated Japanese plant names than readers may be accustomed to. My hope is that this augments the reading experience in a particular way. My hope is that readers will be able to feel, to a certain extent, the kind of disconnect and discomfort Ito describes in being unable to recognize plants in a new language. Just as Ito puzzles over the word "oxalis," so too, readers may puzzle over the word "unohana." There is poetry to be found in this puzzling.

One of the key takeaways from *Tree Spirits Grass Spirits* is that humans and plants have far more in common than we conventionally believe. This is true of names as well. Let me end by addressing one last translation issue: Hiromi Ito's name. In the chapter "Eu-crypta Came Walking," Ito writes about the way her name changes as she moves between Japan and the United States: "I had thought that for humans, there was only one type of existence. Even as I moved to a different country, I still believed this. If I was 'Itō Hi-romi' in Japan, then I would be 'Itō Hiromi' in the United States as well, or worst-case scenario I would be 'Hiromi Ito.'" Readers will notice the writer's "worst case scenario" has become a reality on the cover of this book. But, in this case, the "translation" of the name Itō Hiromi to Hiromi Ito was done at the writer's request. This request, I believe, stems from the vegetal philosophy outlined in *Tree Spirits Grass Spirits*. "Eucrypta Came Walking" continues: "But lately I've been thinking that maybe it might be okay not to have such a unified existence. That maybe it's fine if the Japanese Itō and the American Ito are two different people." And so just as there is *seitaka-awadachisō* and Canadian goldenrod—a single plant that does not live a unified experience across the pacific—so too is there Itō Hiromi and Hiromi Ito. Although they are the same person, this book, in its translated form, is by and about the latter of the two.

TREE SPIRITS GRASS SPIRITS

THE PLANTS IN MY FRONT YARD

Returning to Southern California from Japan early in the new year, I found the sky blue and the air dry and hot at both the Los Angeles airport and the small airport closest to where I live. At the airport in Kumamoto, a light snow had been falling.

My daughter came to welcome me home and told me: "It's been cold up until recently, but the past two or three days have felt like this, with the temperature over eighty degrees." It was eighty-two degrees—Fahrenheit, that is.

I've been living here for close to twenty years. I'm used to the language. Also used to the culture. I am used to the absurd and extreme unit of measurement called Fahrenheit. I no longer think things like: "If it's eighty degrees, then another twenty degrees and it'll be boiling." Eighty degrees in Fahrenheit is around twenty-seven degrees Celsius, which would be a mild heat if it were summer in Japan. But because there is no humidity here, it feels irritating, as if your body fluids are going to evaporate.

When I arrived home, I saw that the young leaves of the nasturtium and the bright green leaves of the oxalis had opened up in the front yard. When I had left home two weeks before, no leaves had sprouted out yet.

I have a front yard that faces the street. It gets the five o'clock sunlight. It gets the western sunlight from the sea. There is no sprinkler system installed. And therefore, it's in ruins. What dies, dies. What survives, survives.

There is a California pepper tree in the middle of the yard. While regular pepper used for cooking belongs to the Piperaceae family, this tree belongs to the Anacardiaceae or cashew family and bears red fruits that hang down in clusters. If you do use it for cooking, it has a fragrance that can become habit forming.

"California" is in the tree's name, and they're everywhere here. They seem like rather old and quite large trees, but they are actually not native to this area. They came from the Andes and then spread. When, several years ago, I bought a young one and planted it, it grew quickly and produced good shade. Like a weeping willow, its delicate leaves hung down and rustled in the wind. One day, I tried hanging flowerpots from its branches. Inside the house (where no air passed through), insects swarmed around the pots. Once they were hung up in the shade where the wind blew, the insects disappeared.

And thus one by one I hung plants from the tree. Now it looks like the front of a shop that makes paper lanterns. There's *Chlorophytum comosum* or spider plant, which is a name easy enough to remember, but there are also plants whose names I can only hear as a kind of incantation or magic spell as I list them off: *Plectranthus, Tradescantia, Nephrolepis, Hoya carnosa, Ceropegia* . . . Standing and chanting the many magical spells belonging to the branches of this still-young pepper tree, concluding with the sacred mantra from the Heart Sutra: *Asplenium, Nematanthus, Aeschynanthus, Gate Gate Paragate* . . . Someday the tree will grow large and bear red fruit that will hang down in clusters.

In front of me stands a *Strelitzia*, also known as a bird-of-paradise. You see them often at flower shops—they're the ones with red flowers that resemble the head of a crane. But the ones in my yard are the kind that grow larger. They grow larger leaves and spread them out haphazardly, and they bloom larger (but not as eye-catching) bluish-black flowers. In the past they were part of the Musaceae family, but they changed the method of classification, and it's now in the Strelitziaceae family. They resemble banana plants, but unlike banana plants, which sprout sloppy leaves from their stalks and lazily spread them out, the leaves of the Strelitziaceae have firm stalks and sprout out one by one from the roots and then stand up and hold their shape. I planted a small one several years ago. It was an impulsive decision. Before I knew it, it had grown large and uncontrollable. I had my regrets, but the bird-of-paradise paid me no mind and continued to grow. And then it continued to grow even more. It grew enormous, like those traveler's trees (which are also of the Strelitziaceae family), where you can see it from far away, its arms spread wide open to welcome me home from my comings and goings.

On the side of the fence: jasmine. And then a rubber tree.

Bugs—scale insects—had gotten into the rubber tree when it was inside the house, and so I planted it in the ground and it grew quickly. Trumpet vines, which you find everywhere here, also protect our fence. Sweet-scented geranium fills in the cracks.

I like sweet-scented geranium. If someone asks me what kind of garden plants I like (well, no one has ever asked me this, so I've never had the chance to answer), I would first say "geranium" and then say "the kind that smells good." And so, this thunderous thicket of sweet-scented geranium brings me joy to no end. Geranium (both the kind that has a fragrance and the kind that doesn't) has a characteristic that resembles octopuses and lizards: if you break off their stems and put them into the ground, just like that you can get as many new ones to emerge as you'd like. The fact that half of my yard is covered in sweet-scented geranium is the result of my patiently continuing to put stems into the ground like this, and the result of their continuing to emerge accordingly. Geranium is a grass, not a tree. Even still, its stems stand up as if it thinks it is a tree and they support each other in growing leaves. The stems are stiff and remain resilient even when the wind blows.

That stiffness is due to the fact that they are carnivorous. Sometimes something dead will fall into a thicket of geranium. A mouse caught in a mouse trap. A sparrow or hummingbird that has smacked into a window. A squirrel that was escaping from a predator but hurt itself and drew its last breath on our property. In the blink of an eye the dead body sinks down into the thicket and, just like that, it is quietly eaten by the sweet-smelling geranium. It doesn't smell like death. A sweet-smelling geranium burial—I think I would like to try that as well.

Come to think of it, euryops are also carnivorous. They are shrubs of the Asteraceae family and bloom yellow flowers. Many years ago, when our cockatiel died, we planted a young euryops on top of where we had buried the bird. We did so because they were the same color. We planted other birds under these roots: the dead body of our budgie, a sparrow that had died in our lawn, a hummingbird that had smashed into a window. As it ate away at these dead bodies, the euryops, with its sturdy trunk, gained strength to bloom its endless flowers.

The flowers of the oxalis have started to bloom. It's still too early for the nasturtium. It hasn't grown fierce enough yet. Surrounded by the nasturtium and the oxalis is sage that should have withered by now but instead has red flowers. The roses that are supposed to be there have disappeared. In a place that the nasturtium and the oxalis can't reach, chamomile and California poppies have started sprouting buds as fine as the hair of a newborn baby. I noticed some green buds growing in the shade of the rubber tree. When I pruned back the tips of the rubber tree, a full daffodil plant appeared. Now it can bathe in the light and bloom its flowers. The toyon I planted two years back will soon dry up. It's a native species here. It's a shrub that grows red fruit and blooms white flowers, but after its last leaf falls it produces no new buds. On its branches are two clumps of red berries that are all shriveling up.

Oxalis. Its full name is *Oxalis pes-caprae*. It's a *katabami* in Japanese or wood sorrel in English—a naturalized plant, as far the land is concerned, originally from South Africa.

When it's called *Oxalis pes-caprae* it sounds like a magic spell, but I'm very familiar with *katabami*. I played with it often when I was a kid. Way back then (in what is called the Shōwa era in Japan), I got used to seeing certain species of plants in the back alleys of Tokyo: non-native species with pink flowers and native species that had yellow flowers and large pods that would set seeds flying. The leaves of the yellow flowers looked like clover, but clover and *katabami* are not of equal value—it's a joy to find clover and a disappointment to find *katabami*. It's easy to tell them apart if their flowers are present, but when there are no flowers, you can tell the difference by the size of the leaves and by the way they are attached to the ground.

There is a native species of *katabami* in North America. It came all the way to Japan and is now called a "naturalized species." Its name in Japanese is *ottachi-katabami*. The word "*ottachi*" is a rather hastily chosen name that comes from an informal way of speaking that means "to be erect." They could have at least used a politer name, but I guess the first impression you get from the plant is the way it stands up straight—a way of standing erect that can only be properly expressed with the vulgarity of the word "*ottachi*." I've only ever seen them in illustrated guides. I've never seen them in either California or Japan. I probably *have* seen some, but I haven't identified any. They are native to North America, but North America is a big place, and they don't grow natively in California.

In photos, they look similar to the native *katabami* of Japan. To be sure, their stems stand up in an erect way that is best described by the expression "*ottachi*." But no matter how erect they are, they can't compare to the standing stalks of *Oxalis pes-caprae*. *Oxalis pes-caprae* stand so erect that you could almost say they are "in heat."

It was in February fifteen years ago that I took my daughters and immigrated to this country. *Oxalis pes-caprae* must have been in bloom back then, but I have no memories of it. Time passed and the following spring arrived, and I saw leaves sprout out and grow dense and perfectly round and assert the immaturity and sweetness of a baby mammal. And then I saw flower stems stand up and begin to bloom yellow flowers.

At first, I didn't know what they were called. Seeing the flowers, it was clear they were *katabami*. But they were bigger than any of the *katabami* I was used to seeing in Japan, and the outline of the flowers stood out in sharper relief. Soon after, I saw some cultivated varieties in a plant shop that looked similar. Some had flowers that were pink and some had leaves that were purple, but they were all named "oxalis." And so, I too began calling this yellow *katabami* an "oxalis."

Well, I say I "called" it oxalis, but I never discussed it with the locals here. So I don't actually know the correct pronunciation to call it "oxalis." Actually, I don't even know if it is really called oxalis in English. A gardener that comes every other week—I say "gardener," but his main job is to clean up the leaves and branches that fall ceaselessly off the eucalyptus trees—hates the plant, and he pulls it up on sight. When a cluster of it was pulled up from our yard, I went out to protest. Since then, he's been wary of me and doesn't touch the oxalis. He called it a "weed." He said, "I pull it up because it's a weed."

Every year it becomes a topic of conversation among my daughters. A conversation they have in Japanese, but one in which they use the word "oxalis": "The oxalis is back, huh?" "I hate the oxalis, don't you?" "Oh, the oxalis is dead, huh?"

Abandoning everything, we left Japan behind. Our family, our house, our relationships with other people, our language. The children had a hard time adapting. We had a hard time getting permanent resident visas. I had a hard time understanding English. I just couldn't get to the point of being able to speak it. I was forgetting Japanese—it felt like sand falling between my fingers. I was worried.

It was then that I saw the plant dyeing our California yard in a bright, soft green. I saw it growing in profusion, looking as if it were about to break out into a sweat. I saw the stems of flowers reaching up and out bravely. Before long, these stems had stood up with all their might, faced the sun, and bloomed yellow flowers. As if they had thought long and hard about it, the flowers bloomed in a dignified manner. The yellow of these flowers was purer than the yellow of acacia or euryops. It was a glassy and rich yellow, like the yolk of an egg.

When its long flowering season comes to an end, oxalis withers all at once, and each one uproots from the soil. But at that point they have already left behind many small radish-like bulbs within the earth. It's a fertility more amazing than that of mice or rabbits. Each bulb sleeps a whole year and then opens its eyes in spring. They grow and spread out their leaves and clump together luxuriantly, blooming dignified yellow flowers. I couldn't help but feel that with their way of life as "naturalized plants," and with that very name, that they were somehow of my own flesh and blood. I had prayed for the kind of aggressive fertility they had, but I only gave birth to three children. I didn't have enough strength. It was disappointing.

It's spring, and so many trees are in full bloom: cherry trees, apple trees, apricot trees, plum trees. We don't have any of these, but they are blooming in the neighborhood. Several are in bloom at the church across the street. They are also blooming at the house of the Nikkei Japanese American who lives in the neighborhood (who sometimes puts out Japanese language newspapers on recycling day).

I am no longer surprised that trees are already in full bloom, but I just cannot get used to the cherry trees reaching full bloom in January. The tall deciduous trees of the Rosaceae or rose family were originally supposed to grow in climates that fluctuated between four seasons. In fall, their leaves would change color; in winter, they endure the cold; in spring, they suddenly bloom flowers. Here there is an everlasting spring with harsh sunlight, where sometimes the warm winds from the desert blow and dry everything up. As their leaves burn, the trees of the Rosaceae family live here uncomfortably. When people plant them in their yards knowing full well it is the wrong climate for them, it's not the trees that draw your attention, but rather a feeling akin to homesickness that is conspicuous.

There is a main thoroughfare that runs through California from north to south. It's called Interstate Highway 5. It runs nearby our house as well. If you get on and drive it for about thirty minutes, you reach the border to Mexico, where it ends. But if you head north, it goes on and on.

How many days would it take to pass through California, and on through Oregon and Washington, and then reach the Canadian border? After you pass through Los Angeles, you enter a valley that's an agricultural zone. You can drive for several hours straight and it still continues on and on. On both sides of the road, fields continue for miles and miles: almond fields, cherry fields, apricot fields, peach fields, plum fields . . . All of those almond trees and most of the rest of them are all tall deciduous trees of the Rosaceae family. They all bloom flowers that resemble cherry blossoms. With almond fields, there is no need to carefully harvest the nuts, so the fields are made up of tall trees. When summer ends, they shake the nuts down with a machine, fill up large containers and carry them off somewhere. Right now, it's surely just flowers, flowers, and more flowers—both sides of the road are surely bright white with flowers.

When the wind blows, the blossoms surely scatter like snow and cover the dry soil below.

Compared to the cherry blossoms in Japan, which are met with wild enthusiasm, these blossoms can't measure up. The scenery is as to be expected for plantations, but my heart stirs just seeing the flowers of these Rosaceae trees blossom and then scatter. It's a stirring feeling that I share with the Nikkei Japanese American neighbor who planted a cherry tree in their yard.

As the flowers of Rosaceae trees meet their end, next up the acacia of the Fabaceae or pea family bloom their flowers. Like eucalyptus, they came from Australia. Like eucalyptus, they have over-adapted and they're everywhere here. Their branches and leaves are overly simple looking, and they usually do not draw attention in any way. But when the flowers of Rosaceae trees come to an end in spring, and after a few rains, all of a sudden thickets of acacia are dyed a bright yellow and their true nature is exposed. Rain and flowers are tied together. Tied with them are memories of a hit song from the 1960s by Nishida Sachiko, with lyrics that go: "I would like to pass away/ being struck by the acacia rain."

But they haven't bloomed yet. Such intense sunlight, and yet the California spring is still young. It hasn't matured to the point of acacias.

EUCALYPTUS TOBACCO PARTY

I continue living a restless life, returning to Southern California in the beginning of January, going to Japan at the end of January, and then coming back to Southern California in the middle of February. I saw California poppies blooming along the roads leading back from the airport. I saw the montbretia that had escaped from a garden in full bloom. The acacia was a yellow beyond yellow. What's more, rain was gently falling, moistening all the plants.

Right away I went to the park next door. Blooming, blooming, blooming, blooming, spring in the wasteland had begun.

You see, rain falls from winter to spring here. From around April, things begin to dry up, and then the dry season continues on and on. There is a severe lack of water, to an extent that would be un-imaginable to the broadleaf evergreens and naturalized plants of Kumamoto in southern Japan. And so the plants of California spend their lives silent.

But right now, and right now only, rain falls here as well. Like the teachings of the Buddha (or so the saying goes), rain falls and moistens all plants equally. The giant pines, the evergreen oaks, the medium-sized yuccas, the cacti, the thickets of sage, the small lichens, the moss—rain moistens each and every one. And then various grasses sprout up from the earth and bloom their flowers. The plants that have endured the dryness bloom flowers—they nurture their various buds as if they were holding them close to their bosoms.

In certain parts of California there are areas designated to protect native plant species. The park next to where I live is the smallest protected area for native plant species in the state. Fourteen years ago, during the summer dry season, I took my dog for a walk and set foot in this area. It was a "wasteland," astonishingly so. Then winter came, and then spring came. Every corner of the wasteland was covered in flowers. It took my breath away.

I couldn't find the names of these plants even when I looked them up in field guides. Even when I did find them, the names weren't in Japanese. I wasn't used to this. I felt uncomfortable. I couldn't get close to these plants.

I would take the dog for a walk in the morning and my daughter would take it in the evening. My daughter, who walked the same course and saw the same grasses and flowers, wanted to be able to talk about the grasses and flowers. So I, on my own, began giving them Japanese names. Words are, after all, a means of communication. As I diligently assigned names that wouldn't make sense to anyone but my daughter, I wandered about the springtime wasteland, feeling like I was the famous botanist Makino Tomitarō, washed up on a deserted island.

Spring in the wasteland begins with "*tōmisō*," which in English means "far-view grass." Actually, I know the real English name. When my friend taught it to me, I resented their meddling. It was a boring name: "monkey flower." *Tōmisō*—it stretches up and blooms within the desolate early spring wasteland in such a way that one can view it from far away.

And then comes the scent of "*jinkōzakura*," which means "incense-cherry tree." *Jinkōzakura*—a small tree with small leaves that blooms fragrant white flowers, just like a cherry tree.

And then "*yama rairakku*," which means "mountain lilac." It actually is called "mountain lilac" in English. It belongs to the Rhamnaceae family, which is quite remote from true lilac (which is of the

Oleaceae family), and it has no scent. But its shape, with its clusters of small flowers, is somehow lilac-esque. At this time of year, the inland mountains are dyed in the color of this flower. To compare it to flowers in Japan, it's like how mountain cherry trees whoosh up into full bloom in spring, or like how mountain wisteria comes to cover the bare mountainsides in early summer—the mountains here are dyed in that type of gentle white and purple.

And then "*se-ji*," or "sage." It's a direct translation from English. To be honest, Southern California is lousy with sage. The purple clumps that grow all over the place here are all sage, although their shapes differ. They belong to the Lamiaceae family, which in Japanese is called the *Shiso* family, and so they eventually bloom flowers that resemble those of the *shiso* plant familiar in Japan. Right now, the new leaves are growing steadily, and forcing out the last year's leaves. As I rub one of the leaves between my fingers, an intense aroma seeps into me.

And then the "*ranseika*," or "egg-laying flower," blooms its flowers. *Ranseika*—I call it this, but its real name is obvious from the shape of its leaves. It's yucca. First, it produces buds that look like eggs that grow within its root stock. Giant eggs that are flesh colored. The leaves of yucca plants, which are sharp enough to injure both humans and animals, carefully protect and nurture these buds. Before long, the eggs start to come apart, and lots of white flowers come rolling out. I can't help but call it "*ranseika*."

Spring in the wasteland deepens. Rain was scarce in the winter, and it caused me to worry, but spring came right on time. "Ah, it's amazing, the rain is amazing"—as I was thinking this, I returned home and noticed something. Something white had blown in and covered the entire backyard. It was eucalyptus flowers. It hadn't been like this two weeks ago when I left for Japan.

There are five big eucalyptus trees in my backyard. Because they continuously shed their leaves, branches, and bark, we constantly get complaints from the neighbors. My husband feigns complete ignorance of this fact.

In Japanese we call eucalyptus *"yu-kari."* The English word comes from Latin, where *"eu"* means "well" or "good," and *"calyptus"* means "covered." Put another way, the plant's name is derived from how the calyx and flower petals adhere to and cover over the whole flower. When it comes time for them to bloom, this covering comes off and flowers appear—they're unique flowers. Picture a feijoa flower. Huh? You don't know it? Ok then, an acacia flower, not the fake acacia known as "black locust," but a real acacia—can you picture it? The kind that tends to die off in the rain. What, you don't know that one either? In that case, it's ok to imagine the more familiar flower of the silk tree. You know, that type of soft, fluffy flower.

What looks like a flower petal is actually a stamen. Stamen—a reproductive organ, dozens of which sprout out and stand tall, pretending to be flowers. Before long, the flowers fall. In vast numbers. They pile up on the ground and are driven together by the wind and rain.

In my neighborhood there is a park called Cottonwood Creek Park, where a small river they call a "creek" runs through it, and where many trees called "cottonwoods" (which resemble *"nekoyanagi"* or "rose-gold pussy willow" trees) grow wild along the edge of the creek. In the back of the park stand tall and robust eucalyptus trees, magnificent with red flowers. They are too tall for us to see their flowers when in bloom, but the ground around the trees is covered in flowers that fall. I went thinking it might be the flowering season, but nothing had fallen to the ground. What in the world? Since long ago I had thought this plant called eucalyptus was somehow an unpredictable plant.

For starters, the flowering season is random, like I said. It seems to vary by type, or by individual tree.

And the leaf shape is also random. It differs between young and established trees, and even the same type of tree differs by location, like with trees that have been grafted. You might think everything is this way, but that's not so. There are things that remain consistent. What's more, the bark of the tree peels off to an excessive degree. Of course, there are ones that don't shed their bark at all. The bark that doesn't peel off piles up in a scraggily, unrefined way, as if it has a slow metabolism. The trees that do shed bark shed too much and get dull-looking and slippery.

And they shed branches as well. They peel off and fall to the ground. Sometimes a giant branch that looks like it could crush a person comes roaring down mercilessly. I used to think that trees grew by branching out, and then branching out again, but euca-lyptus trees shed their branches right after they grow and rapidly fling them around. Each tree has large branches full of flowers and leaves that hang down dangerously.

Speaking of which, here's something that happened long ago. A Mexican couple appeared suddenly at my door, and asked if they could have some eucalyptus leaves, to which I said, "Sure!" The cou-ple then grabbed a tall ladder and, using a machine, started cutting and then steadily carrying off the fallen leaves and branches, and without paying any attention to any of the other trees, made that one tree completely bald within moments, and then headed out. The leaves of the other trees were long and narrow, but the leaves of the tree they cut from were silver and round. I tried to imagine what they were going to use them for. Maybe filler for bouquets sold in a flower shop? Maybe they would refine it for eucalyptus oil? If you were to ask a vendor to trim a tree like that, it would cost 200,000 or 300,000 Japanese yen (or about two to three thousand US dollars). It was on the edge of the property and was the type that had an excessively strong metabolism, with leaves and branches long and narrow like a willow that frequently fell into the neighbor's yard. Every time a complaint came from the neighbors, I wondered whether that couple might return, but they never came again.

I live my life enclosed within eucalypti. This tree of Australian origin has infested Southern California. Even now, whenever I see one, I feel uncomfortable. The way they stand, the way they peel, their leaves, flowers, all of it. I feel this way because of the randomness, the fact that you can't get to know the tree's true nature. Or so I think, as a diligent and prim Japanese person. Yet at the same time, it's not as if I don't get the feeling that I've actually known their true nature since long ago.

This might be because eucalyptus trees have certain elements that resemble trees that I am familiar with. For example, if you look at the leaves, they resemble willow trees. They're tall, and that part of them that rustles in the wind way up above the sky resembles poplar trees. Their leaves are oily, and that part of them that creates a strong aroma resembles camphor trees.

Considering their origins in Australia, it seems quite alright that I want to call them something like "owl willow," or "owl poplar," or "owl camphor," as the Japanese words for both sugar glider and quoll use the word for owl, *fukurō*. I'll share with you a memory, without resorting to such silly talk.

Long ago, an Australian man proposed to me. Invited by the local university, Aboriginal artists from Australia came to make drawings in their characteristic dotted style.

One of them said, "Fill it in from the edges. White people will make an island of dots and then make another one in another spot, and then start filling in the space in-between. But it takes too much effort that way." They continued, "You gain strength by continually making the dots. Strength steadily builds if you start from the edges, and you can reach the whole circumference."

The university, like just about everywhere else in Southern California, was full of eucalyptus trees. The artists gathered up tree bark incessantly when they came. But not the bark of just any tree—only from particular eucalyptus trees, it seemed. Then that night, in the yard of a house that was throwing a party, they began burning the bark. One of the artists took a liking to me. He asked, in faltering English, "You will marry me?" (He was a fairly old man. It seemed as if he had received English education later on in life.) "No, I won't marry you," I responded in faltering English. (I was still very bad at English.) Then he said something like, "You're kidding me!" and wrapped me up in his arms and forcibly kissed me.

I had a brief thought: "Maybe it would be okay to stay like this, forever making dots." I was thirty-five years old and had just come all the way to California after drifting through life aimlessly.

Of all the people at the party, only I was invited to the artists' eucalyptus tobacco session. It was an honor. We exited the yard, and together with the men I chewed on the ashes of the eucalyptus tree bark—we mixed it with tobacco and chewed. It was rough. While chewing, the eucalyptus circled through me. I wanted to throw up. I couldn't handle it, and without saying goodbye to the man who proposed to me, hurried back home. Of course, I drove myself home. I'm someone who doesn't really get into accidents. When I got to my room, I could no longer stand up, and I threw up all night long, writhing in pain. The world was just spinning around me, and I had no hallucinations or sense of euphoria—only discomfort. That stuff, that's what koalas eat.

Immediately the following day, my suitor returned to Australia. I missed my chance to get married, but I don't regret getting to know that eucalyptus poison firsthand.

THE BLACK MONK CARRIES
A GLOSSY PARASOL

Having come all the way to California, I yearned, for a long, long time, for the trees, bushes, and vines of the broadleaf evergreen forest zone of East Asia. I yearned for the aster called *miyakowasure* (or "forget-the-capital") and the primrose called *sakurasō* (or "cherry tree grass"), both of which used to be grown in plastic pots along the back alleys of Tokyo. I yearned for the ferns which grew up over walls with no restraint, as well as the *gibōshi* (plantain lilies) and the *tsuwabuki* (leopard plant).

There was an old well behind the house I lived in as a child. There was an oak tree that dropped acorns around, and there was a fig tree, and irises bloomed in damp spots, and ginger and *myoga* (Japanese ginger) grew rampant. *Shiso* and taro were being grown in the field across the way. And so, even here in California, I gathered decorative plants for the interior of my home, and tried to transform this dry, desert-like zone into the broadleaf evergreen forest zone. Instead of taro, I raise things in the same family like *Monstera*, *Alocasia*, and *Anthurium*, and instead of *shiso*, I naturally raise things in the same family like *Glechoma* and *Plectranthus*, and instead of ginger and *myoga*, I raise things that slightly resemble the ginger family, like *Calathea* and *Ctenanthe*, which are both of the arrowroot family.

I know it's impossible. When I go outside, the sunlight beats down blindingly. The sky always shines bright blue. And rain is decidedly scarce. There is a drought come summer about every other year, and I can't help but walk around in a daze. An order comes down from on high: "In order to conserve water, stop watering plants! If you absolutely have to water them, do so at night."

So people stop growing plants that need a lot of water and they grow Aloaceae, they grow Euphorbiaceae, they grow Agavaceae, they grow Cactacae—they grow what are commonly referred to as succulents. They don't need water. They take no effort. Leave them alone, and new bulbs emerge and shoot up, increasing one after the other. They even bloom flowers. Many beautiful, solid color flowers. But, how can I put it . . . They're boring.

They're interesting to look at when you go to the desert. Their flowers bloom in spring there. Around here, all of nature is a desert. The further inland you go, the better the weather gets, and the more intense and bright the sunlight gets, and the more the blue of the sky stands out. And the atmosphere gets drier. The English word "desert" calls to mind images of sand. But it's not just sand, there are plants growing: Asteraceae (daisies), Lamiaceae (mint), and all kinds of succulents. More than just growing, they're actually overflowing. Succulent leaves are usually unremarkable and green, but these ones are often grey or yellowish green. Not much different than the color of dust. But despite this, when it rains and spring arrives, they bloom freshly colored flowers all at once. My, how delightful it is.

But succulents in gardens are boring. You can't touch them freely because they often have thorns and are poisonous. Like with a cat that is overly afraid of people and won't come out of the closet, it's boring not being able to caress or embrace them. But when spring arrives so does their flowering season. Their blooms are just as pretty as regular flowers, and sometimes, even more vibrant, perhaps even miraculous.

There's a plant here that caught my interest. Its shape looks as if its large, fully-crowned head is mounted on top of a slender neck. The neck is its stem, the head is made of its leaves. The leaves line up like the shape of a lotus flower. There are ones with green leaves and ones with black leaves. The shape is strange, but so too is this black color—because it is such a dark black, you catch a glimpse of them here and there as you go about your daily routine, driving around bright, ordinary residential areas. They are *Aeonium arboreum*, of the Crassulaceae family. The one with the black head, or rather the one with black leaves, is named "*kurohōshi*" in Japanese, which means "black monk."

The green-headed one has the same Latin name, but a completely different Japanese name: it's called "*tsuyabigasa*," or "glossy parasol."

With only a difference in color, why is it that the impression given by these names is so different? And why, in the first place, are both names written in *kanji* or Chinese characters, rather than in the phonetic *katakana* characters that are used to write foreign words and scientific terminology?

In Japanese, plant names are usually in *katakana*. *Akinokirinsō, seitaka-awadachisō, miyakowasure, yōshuyamagobō, seitaka-daiō*—all of these are faithfully written in *katakana*. And it is because these plants all have names written in *katakana* that they are able to live in a plant-like way, and therefore we can have peace of mind and treat them as plants. But for some reason, succulents (and succulents only) are allowed to have names written in strange kanji characters. Too strange—names like those of *yōkai* monsters in comics for young boys. Like *tekkōmaru* (written as "iron helmet") and *daiginryū* (written as "big silver dragon"), both of the Agavaceae family. Or *ryūkaku* ("dragon horn"), *gyūkaku* ("cow horn"), and *amanojaku* ("mischievous demon"), all of the Asclepiadaceae family. *Kumadōji* ("bear child") and *tsukitoji* ("moon-rabbit ears"), both of the Crassulaceae family. If you were to look hard enough, there are probably ones with names like *Inuyasha* (like the famous cartoon of the same name) or *shikon-no-tama* (or "jewel of four souls," from the same cartoon). I figure this penchant for *kanji* is a relic of the early modern Edo period, when kanji were more beloved, but I have no proof of this. I'll do some research.

Anyway, "black monk," of the Crassulaceae family. The Japanese name of this family is *benkeisōka*, which if written in *kanji* bears the name of a famous warrior monk. Right now, in California, at the full peak of its bloom: this plant which spreads an ominous feeling, like Musashibō Benkei or Hitachibō Kaison might have, those two warrior monks who wore black headgear (apparently called *katō*), as was typical at the end of the ancient Heian period. Flower stems stick out from the center of the black, blooming a profuse amount of bright yellow flowers that look just like chrysanthemums. "Black monk, don't give in to the sins of the flesh!" Just looking at it, my heart pounds.

There is another succulent that weighs heavily on my mind. This one too, right now, is in full bloom.

It's a big one. It's not tall, but it's an armful, sometimes two armfuls. Many vibrant, blue, fleshy leaves overlap and form a "calyx" like that of a lotus flower. However, flower stems weave their way out from the center of the calyx and extend one to two meters, drawing an arc and hanging downward. Because it's surrounded by small flowers, from far away it looks soft and fluffy like a canine tail. These are planted in what pass for yards around here. Here and there calyxes group together, extend out their flower stems, and hang their long tails. It's too strange, and for a moment you fall into a feeling like: "Where am I?"

It's *Agave attenuata*, of Mexican origin, related to agave or *ryūzetsuran*. In *kanji*, this plant's name means "dragon-tongue orchid."

Ryūzetsuran is a romantic name when written in kanji. But because its taxonomical family is also *ryūzetsuran* (Agavaceae in English), this name also makes use of *katakana* characters.

Because Mexico's right there, the climate of Southern California works perfectly for agave. And that shape, if you ask me, that's what makes it agave—many thick leaves overlapping each other and forming a calyx. As the rootstock ripens, stems rise up, weaving their way from the center, and bloom flowers. Those parts surely make it an agave. But its leaves do not have the thorns typical of plants in the Agavaceae family. "*Attenuata*" means "without adornment." In addition, agaves typically form calyxes that emerge abruptly up from the ground, but *Agave attenuata* have short stalks under their calyx. It looks like the plant's neck. It looks like a heavy head has climbed atop a short, thick neck that resembles that of a boar.

Living here, one gets extremely well acquainted with agave. After all, they are native here. The mountains around my home are full of rocks. In spring, something that resembles white field horsetails spring up one after the other all over the rocky slopes. It looks like field horsetail from far away, but if you look at it close up, you'll see that they're yuccas that have grown stems and bloomed flowers. No matter how small their rootstocks might be, there are some that grow as tall as humans. Although the Japanese name for Agavaceae (*ryūzetsuran-ka*) has the word for orchid (*ran*) in it, it is not in the Orchidaceae (or orchid) family. Yucca flowers do look a lot like orchids, however. Fleshy, brilliant, and white. Because they clump together at the tips of long stems, they look like field horsetail from far away.

Forcing one's way inland, one reaches a point where the rocky wasteland gets more desolate and even more brutal. Here grows an awe-inspiring agave that is larger than the yucca—a variety called *Agave americana*.

Agave americana: "century plant" in English. The name comes from the popular belief that they only bloom flowers once a century. To be exact, it's just that it grows slowly and doesn't mature easily. When it does mature, it blooms flowers, and then its roots dry out.

We have one in our backyard as well. A long time back, we received it from a friend on my husband's birthday. One day, a gardener came over and dug a hole right in the middle of the backyard, and then planted the large, adult *Agave americana* (it seems that in the past, gardeners in this area used to be of Japanese descent, but now they are usually Mexican). I thought that the plant might have been around ninety years old at the time.

For about the span of ten years, the agave continued to produce new bulbs here and there. It stretched its roots out underground, and ended up multiplying in unexpected places. It created new bulbs all over our not-so-wide backyard. It's an overbearing plant; even the small ones have a large build to them. They have sharp leaves, so you can't absentmindedly get too close to them. It was a total nuisance. The young bulbs were the same shape as the parent bulb, and had sharp leaves just like it. I trembled thinking of what was to come.

Yet in spite of this, they had that strange charm characteristic of young things, and I couldn't bring myself to throw them away rashly. It's a charm that resembles that of kittens and puppies. I thought I would dig them up and move them to another place, but because they would cause trouble if they spread in the new spot, I couldn't plant them in just any old place. So I grew them in pots and gave them away to people. I took diligent care of the bulbs that I had planted in pots. It was as if I was tirelessly searching for people to take kittens that kept being born one after another. Although you can solve the kitten problem by spaying or neutering the parent cat, you cannot spay or neuter an agave. Before long, things got out of hand and I started neglecting them. So now the backyard is covered in agaves, in a state that resembles an agave kindergarten. Thankfully they mature slowly, so when I take one out of the ground, I see that none of them have yet reached puberty. But the one I removed has already started multiplying and is covered in many small bulbs.

The parent bulb that we had first received stretched out a large stem and bloomed flowers in exactly its one-hundredth year (or so I wanted to think). The end of the stem branched out and produced yellow flowers. They were flowers I noticed often in the wasteland. They were stems and flowers that you could always find in landscape photos of this area. When the flowers came to an end, the bulb dried up and died. The spot where the dried-up bulb had been is now wide open.

Let me return to talk of the *attenuata*, that plant with a vibrant green calyx. I received a new bulb of one from a friend's house. A new bulb small enough to fit in the palm of my hand. I immediately planted it in the front yard. While it's hard work dealing with sharp agaves, this plant has no thorns, so it was easy to plant. That was already several years ago. It hasn't gotten the least bit larger. I read somewhere that it takes decades for them to bloom in full. This small agave won't bloom until it passes around the same amount of days as I have since immigrating to this land fifteen years ago.

The bulbs of these *attenuata*—which hang down their curious flowers here and there around town—will all, before long, die. If they were human, they'd be elderly people close to one hundred years old. They will, before long, die—but it's not sad. Up until this point, they've made new bulbs to their hearts' content. Each new bulb is the spitting image of its parent bulb. Their death is neither sad nor painful. It's not even the end.

I think as I gaze at them: dogs and humans "grow old and die," but for plants, "dying" is "not dying," and "not dying" is "living," right? This is the karma unique to them and them alone.

GRASS, WILDFLOWERS

I boarded a small plane to Los Angeles at the small airport nearest me, changed there to a large plane to Narita Airport, from Narita a bus to Haneda Airport, from Haneda board another plane and finally reached Kumamoto. It was an afternoon flight. Looking down from the plane, I noticed several clusters of white on the surface of the ground as the plane drew closer to the land past the Aso mountain range. I thought it was a field of *susuki* or Japanese pampas grass. But no, I could tell from the condition of the clusters that while it resembled *susuki*, it was like a much larger type of pampas grass. It was already April, and so it seemed like they were all dried out, with fluffy heads of white. Pampas grass—this grass is showy and looks like a male silverback gorilla. But it's too fertile and at some point goes beyond its capabilities. Sooner or later, it takes off and endangers the plants that rise up from the soil, and then you run the risk of having to cut it down and kill it every time you see it. Why, I wonder, in spite of all of this, would someone plant such a thing, but as my plane touched down, I began thinking: "Wrong, totally wrong. It's not pampas grass, could this much pampas grass grow in Japan, a place where *susuki* grows native in the first place? Those many clusters of white I see are much bigger than the likes of old pampas grass plants."

Then I recognized them. They were *sakura*. They were cherry trees in full bloom. Because I saw them from the sky, I had been confused about their size. Blooming flowers wrapped the cherry trees up, covering plots of land both near and far. They covered the areas along both sides of the roads, which were busy with the coming and going of cars; they covered the circumference of a large park; they covered the gardens outside people's homes; they covered the area within the mountain forest near the airport. And then the plane landed. Heading into the city, I left the blooming trees behind. They had been more vague than beautiful. They existed only within the realm of consciousness, with no real substance.

Well, all things must pass. The leaves of the cherry trees increased day by day. Now the trees are all full of leaves. Delicate white flowers are buried in green. To be sure, it's a dreadful thing, but what interests me now sits underfoot. It's the grass that grows in clumps at one's feet, the grass that gets called "weeds" or "wildflowers."

However, as someone with age-induced farsightedness, there is nothing as difficult to make out as the grass beneath my feet. I try, with cloudy eyes, to differentiate each flower, one by one, and each stem, one by one, and the way leaves emerge from the stalks—how could it be so difficult? Differentiating one by one, identifying each name—how difficult it is! Based on the colors of the flowers or shapes of the leaves that I somehow manage to differentiate, I guess the scientific family name and look them up one after another. Sooner or later I figure it out.

I look them up and look them up again, but there's always more. I figure out one type of grass and with no time to even sigh with relief, thoughts of another grass that I have yet to identify come clawing their way out. I don't know where these thoughts come from. They must come from the grass itself.

The purplish-red wildflower called *hotoke-no-za* ("henbit dead-nettle" in English), which up until recently had bloomed in abundance, is almost all gone. *Karasu-no-endō* ("common vetch" in English), which is the same color as *hotoke-no-za*, is also already at the end of its season. Right now, in their place, *suzume-no-endō* ("tiny vetch" in English), with their small, bluish flowers and delicate leaves, are stretching out their tendrils and covering over everything.

It was a while back that I noticed a flower that looks just like forget-me-nots (*wasurenagusa* in Japanese, which means the same thing). The smallness of this flower is a thing of wonder—it's as if some magical power was stirred while the forget-me-not (with its vivid azure hue and bright yellow center) was carried along from Europe to the Far East and then shrunk down to this size. Because I can't see this cute little flower all that well with my aged, farsighted eyes, I think to myself, "Next time I'll head out with my reading glasses"—but I always forget. Year after year, I have gazed at this flower without knowing its name, all the while thinking: "Oh how cute! Oh how pretty!" But the other day, I finally identified it. Pinning it down, I found out it's called *kyūrigusa* (which translates as "cucumber grass" and goes by the name cucumber herb in English)—a very ordinary-sounding name. While forget-me-nots have a poetic name, this flower is just called cucumber grass—what the heck? But sometimes even the English names for plants are like this one, which is called a cucumber even though it's not a cucumber. In general, the etymology comes from the smell. Could it be that in both Japanese and English, in the consciousness of people in the distant past, the scent of cucumber was so memorable and vivid?

They say cucumber grass is a naturalized plant. Even so, they say it's an ancient naturalized plant, one that came around the same time as the ancestor of barley. How in the world could we call this a "naturalized plant?" Is it right to do so? If it were humans we were talking about, wouldn't they already be considered fellow countrymen? As a humble immigrant myself, this is a question I can't let go of.

There is a type of grass that resembles cucumber grass but is even smaller and harder to see. When I picked some and brought it home, and then looked at it with my glasses on—oh, how blue and lovely. But it soon wilted and I couldn't put it in water. I thought it might be that one called *hanaibana* and so I looked it up, but of course I was wrong. What I hit upon after a long search was *nojisha*.

Nojisha—where the "no" can be written with the Chinese character for "field." In English it's "lamb's lettuce," in French it's called "mâche." In California, it's been cultivated to be large and easy to eat, and it gets packaged and sold for use in salads. It's sweet and tender, and it's good in salads or in soup broth. So I picked a bit of this *nojisha* and tasted it. It had the same flavor. The packaged kind is ten times bigger and doesn't have any flowers. That kind is a vegetable, this kind is grass. It's all over the place. And so it's probably covered in dog pee. But if you picked it all, you could have quite the supply of food.

My interest in plants originally began when I was child, the consequence of an imaginary thought that served as the core of my life at the time: how to survive if the planet were destroyed. This is all I thought about in that period of time before hitting puberty. First my parents die, then school is destroyed—how to survive in that situation. Over and over I imagined it. First my parents die, then school is destroyed—the world falls into ruins. It was as if my parents dying and school being destroyed were the foundation of my fantasy. I was convinced that I would never be free unless those things happened. I had to acquire the daily skills necessary to survive once my parents died and school was destroyed. In order to secure a food supply, I began closely examining the plants around me.

That habit remains to this day, and I'm always thinking as I walk around: "This is edible. That over there is edible too. Boil it in soy sauce, or pickle it and eat it. I could even eat chrysanthemum flowers or fatsia sprouts if I fried them as tempura." I suddenly realized there was a problem in thinking that all kinds of things could be fried as tempura—in the wake of my parents dying and school being destroyed, setting aside the grass for a moment, how would I be able to procure things like flour, oil, salt, and soy sauce? I realized this as a child, and I've been thinking about it ever since. I still don't have a solution.

Since around that time, I have known the plant name *ōinu-no-fuguri*. Naturally, for a child, the word "*fuguri*" (which means testicles) had an unforgettable impact, even if it referred to a dog's testicles ("*ōinu*" means "large dog"). And so I remembered the name easily. I thought it was related to that stuff called *he-kuso-kazura* that blooms in summer. Related by name, that is—"*he-kuso-kazura*" translates as "fart-shit arrowroot." That, too, has come to the end of its season. How to describe the blue of its flower ... maybe like a glassy, mixed blue? It's a shiny, shiny blue, so shiny that it makes you worry about your eyes when you stare at it.

I had somehow thought that there seemed to be two types of *hakobe* (or "chickweed" in English). There's the small kind that creeps along the ground, with soft leaves and stems that seem sweet if you were to chew on them, with white petals all lined up in sharp relief, looking like fluttering eyelashes, and there's the kind with stems that grow unsteadily and bloom flowers that leave a sharp, spiny impression. However, on this occasion, as I rubbed my farsighted eyes and looked closely to see why they seemed spiny, I saw that the petals were long and narrow, and that each one was split in two. I did some research and quickly figured it out. The kind that was small and stood out in sharp relief was regular old *hakobe*, the kind with petals that split in two and looked spiny was *oranda-miminagusa* (which translates as "Dutch ear grass," but is called "sticky mouse-ear chickweed" in English).

I cannot tell the difference between *suzume-no-katabira* ("annual bluegrass" in English) and *niwahokori* ("Indian lovegrass" in English). I knew the name *niwahokori* (which translates as "yard dust") as a child, and like *yabugarashi* (dried thicket) and *noborogiku* (tattered-rag field chrysanthemum), I admired how the name was full of emotion (as well as bad connotations). Ever since then, whenever I've seen a similar-looking grass of the Poaceae family, I've continued to be impressed, thinking to myself: "Ahh, it's the dust of the yard." But a few years ago, I learned there is a grass called *suzume-no-katabira* (which translates as "sparrow robe") that looks just like *niwahokori*. I also learned that I simply cannot tell them apart. It would cause me distress if someone were to tell me that what I've been seeing is not the dust of the yard but rather the robe of a sparrow. I truly want to just let it go on being *niwahokori*.

There's more. Ordinary *yomogi* ("mugwort" in English) and *kawara-yomogi* (capillary wormwood), and *himemukashi-yomogi* (horseweed) and *seitaka-awadachisō* (Canadian goldenrod)—all of these are still immature and full of a youthful vibrancy. When summer comes, they'll get fierce and grow luxuriously all over the place. The clover crowds together and will fatten up from here on out. The Carolina geranium is just about to start blooming small pink flowers from its leaves that look just like those of regular geranium. *Odorikosō* (white dead nettle), *suiba* (sorrel), and *uma-no-ashigata* (tall buttercup) steadily multiply. And then, the *yaemugura* (sticky-willy), which grows rampant in an incoherent manner, leans up against the walls and fences. There's more. There's so, so many more.

Tachi-inu-no-fuguri ("common speedwell" in English) has stems that stand up straight one by one. They grow flowers on their tops, but as the sunlight gets dim in the evening, they close up. Their flowers are smaller than those of *kyūrigusa* or *nojisha*, and I can't see them well with my farsighted eyes. There is a section of the Lotus Sutra called "The Parable of the Medicinal Herbs" that goes like this: "Small roots, small stems, small branches, and small leaves. Medium roots, medium stems, medium branches, and medium leaves. Big roots, big stems, big branches, and big leaves." I realize that the "small roots, small stems, small branches, and small leaves" that it mentions must be something like these grasses.

There's *ōinu-no-fuguri* and there's *tachi-inu-no-fuguri*.

Actually, in California, there's *aka-inu-no-fuguri*. From here on out, this will be a story of Californian flowers. It's a story of flowers that are unfamiliar in Japan, so please listen carefully.

They bloom in the wasteland. They cover the ground. They bloom red flowers of a gentle texture that look just like those of *ōinu-no-fuguri* but are not as transparent. Numerous among the plants that cover the ground of the Southern Californian wasteland at this time of year are those of the Onagraceae family. Yellow flowers that resemble a shrunken version of evening primrose bloom all over. Among these, *aka-inu-no-fuguri* is somewhat different.

When I first noticed it, I was excited and reported to my daughters: "There's a flower blooming that's similar to *ōinu-no-fuguri*! It's salmon pink, and it's so cute!"

I couldn't seem to identify it, however. It was similar to *ōinu-no-fuguri*, but I couldn't find it within the Scrophulariaceae family. Its leaves were similar to *hakobe*, but it wasn't anywhere in the Caryophyllaceae family. It creeps along the ground, so maybe in the Onagraceae family? It has cute flowers, so maybe in the Boraginaceae family? I searched high and low, but couldn't find it. And then one day, there was suddenly a picture that was dead on. Reaching this moment—please imagine just how much time I had spent on the internet, how many pictures I had stared at, and just how happy I was once I found it. It's *Anagallis arvensis*, commonly called "scarlet pimpernel." Believe it or not, it belongs to the Primulaceae family, and is a naturalized plant with its origins in Europe.

I had heard the name "scarlet pimpernel" somewhere before. I remembered: it was an old English adventure novel, one that has long been translated into Japanese as *Kurenai hakobe* (or "Scarlet *hakobe*"). And so this grass is called *akabana-ruri-hakobe* in Japanese. There is also, apparently, a grass of the same family and genus that is just called *ruri-hakobe*. That one lives up to its name, as *ruri* means "deep blue," and it seems to have made it to Japan.

It's a mixed-up, unthinkable destiny to be named *akabana* despite not being in the *akabana* (Onagraceae) family; to be named *hakobe* despite not being a *hakobe*; to be named *ruri* despite not being of the color *ruri* (deep blue)—but I secretly call it *aka-inu-no-fuguri*, so who am I to say?

LIVING TREES AND DYING TREES

A large tree in my neighborhood died in early spring. I wasn't sure whether I should say that it had died, or that it had been killed, or that it had been cut down. To me, it was a big event. For a while, I couldn't bring myself to talk about it. I've only just now come around to feeling ready to do so.

It was a pepper tree. A California pepper tree of the Anacardi-aceae family. It has "California" in the name, so naturally there are plenty of them growing around here. You see them all the time, so they're easy to recognize. With coarse bark and leaves that hang down like willows or ferns, they develop clusters of small red ber-ries. The one in my neighborhood had grown large and thick and its branches hung down over the road.

The tree was always there. I admired it every time I passed by. The word "luxuriant" came to mind, written with the Chinese characters for "melancholy" and "blue." The tree created a melancholic shade that made just about everything look blue. Whenever I passed by it, I would remember the voice of Mei, the young girl from the an-imated film *My Neighbor Totoro*, and how she called a row of trees "a tree tunnel." As soon as I would think this, my children would say "a tree tunnel" in unison, imitating Mei. My husband would always say: "It takes about a hundred years to grow that much." He, too, had lived close to a hundred years, and thus he felt an affinity for the tree as he said this.

In short, it was a tree that each member of my family had become attached to in our own way. It stood in front of a few small houses. Rental homes with no yards or fences. They were hidden in the shade of the tree. The tree, which was larger than these homes, was always there, its branches hanging down over the road in a luxurious manner.

It was an early morning in spring when my daughter went outside and called out: "The tree's been cut!"

It was all so sudden that it didn't seem real. A feeling came over me, reminding me that I was aware that things like this could happen. I had had this experience many times before, in many places, and I was never able to do anything about it. I had felt bad, many times over, about not being able to help the dying trees.

I tried making up a story: "The tree had fallen ill and was beginning to rot." We had, a long time ago, cut down a pine tree for this very reason. I tried another story: "It was pressing against the power lines, so the city took action and cut it down." That the residents considered the tree a nuisance, or even hated it—this was the hardest explanation to consider.

"Should we ask someone about it?" asked Tomé, my youngest.

"But it's not really something we can ask anyone about, is it?" replied Sarako, the older of the two.

That evening the sky was pink. To both the east and west, it was brilliantly colored. I took the dogs for a walk up to where the tree had been. We had walked here often in the past. Back then, the dogs were young, and I took them out every day. There were two houses that had dogs along the way. We always got barked at. My dogs were young and reckless, and when they got barked at by dogs they didn't know, they barked right back without caring that they were probably in someone else's territory. This time, too, we got barked at, but my dogs (who had once, long ago, been young) had now become feeble granny dogs. They no longer cared about dogs they didn't know. Since our dogs didn't react to them, you could hear the other dogs' barking begin to mellow out. As a result, I realized that what I had thought was a voice meant to intimidate was actually just showing off—a voice calling out: "Look at me! Look!" There were many acacias along the path. Each one was in bloom. The oxalis, too, spread out all over. It was evening, so the flowers were closed up. There were lawns where succulents had been planted. There was a creeping geranium, its flowers in bloom, climbing up a fence, with no end in sight.

The tree was gone. Bright light stretched out over the road. It was now thoroughly empty. The branches and trunk had been pulverized, seemingly put through a chipper shredder. Several Mexican men were cleaning up the wood chips. Perhaps they were the ones who lived near the tree, or perhaps they had just been hired to help cut it down.

All traces of the tree had gone. In the spot where it had once stood was now a dense pile of fine sawdust that resembled sand. It was a small spot, about the size of three tatami mats. I thought it was miraculous that such a giant tree could grow out of such a small spot and support itself. The sidewalk had been vigorously torn up. At my feet were fallen leaves, which were scattered over the sidewalk and the road. They fell the moment the tree was cut down. As the felled tree was dragged down and cut apart, its leaves spread all around.

For a while after this happened to the tree, I was sad, and I stopped going down that road. And then after a short while I returned to Japan. I spent most of spring in Kumamoto. My oldest daughter Kanoko, who was pregnant at the time, came along with her husband as well. I took them to the town of Takamori in Aso,

as I wanted to show them the giant tree there. This is the story of
a living tree.

Takamori sits at the foot of Mount Aso in Kumamoto. It's only
forty minutes from the Kumamoto Airport. There are houses and
crop fields. There are sources here and there where water wells
up. There are ugly sources that have been used up for commercial
purposes, and there are ones that resemble communal wells that
the local people use in their everyday lives. If you travel a little way,
you'll find one lying quietly in a space between the trees. The water
is completely green in color due to the trees' reflection in the water's
surface. A moss-covered statue of the water god sticks out in the
middle of the water's surface. If you peer inside, you can see that
the bottom of the lake is densely covered in moss, and that fish are
moving around down there. Water springs up all over the place.
There are sources were the water flows from where it bubbles up.
There are also sources where the water trickles down from where it
has climbed up, like from the side of a mountain cliff.

Oh, wait, this wasn't meant to be a story about water. It's a story
about trees. In Takamori, there is an old cherry tree. It is called
the Isshingyō: a name suggesting that it "wholeheartedly" (*isshin*)
practiced the "austerities" (*gyō*) of someone holy. It seems to be a
tree loaded with such meaning. Nearby there also stands a large
sugi, or cedar tree, called the Takamoridono no sugi.

And so, en route from picking up Kanoko and her husband from
the airport, we went to go see the Isshingyō cherry tree. It was past
its flowering season. The loud and chaotic cherry blossom festival
that is held right in the middle of flowering season was over, and
the festival stalls and dance stage had only recently been taken
down and cleared away. The cherry tree was all leaves. I've read
somewhere that the difference between the *yamazakura* variety of
cherry tree and the *somei-yoshino* variety is that once the latter loses

its flowers, it grows leaves, whereas the flowers and red buds of the former variety sprout out at the same time.

Kanoko, who was pregnant, held hands with her husband, and they walked around the large cherry tree. Instead of looking at the scraggly cherry blossoms that remained on the aged branches, they looked down toward the flowers that bloomed plentifully around the old cherry tree's roots: violets, veronica plants, tiny and common vetches. Kanoko spoke to her husband, saying: "These really bring me back to when I was a kid . . ."

On the way back I wondered whether we'd have time to stop by the giant *sugi*. Just thirty minutes up the road that runs in front of the giant cherry tree, you end up at a spot where a small sign stands modestly on the side of the road, as if it's meant to be passed by without being noticed. There is a small gate on the path. It's closed. You open it up and go inside. The gate is meant to keep cows from running away. Inside the gate, there is cow dung everywhere. Of course, it feels like you'll end up stepping in some. Up ahead is a stand of trees, luxuriant, damp, and dark. The kind of place where you'd get bitten by mosquitos in summer. Covered all over with vines, ferns, and moss. If you force your way in there, that's where it is—the giant *sugi*. It splits in two from the roots. It stretches upwards, halts, and then hangs down. One of these days it will completely envelop itself within itself. It will also completely envelop those of us looking up at it. It's that kind of tree.

But no matter how much I ran the numbers, we just didn't have the time. Kanoko and her husband had just arrived in Kumamoto, and I had to bring the pregnant one home to rest. Just as we were leaving for the day, my father seemed to be feeling unwell, so I also had to hurry back to his place. The plan was to show Kanoko and her husband around Aso in three days' time. I thought we could look at the water and the mountain's crater and go to the hot springs. We could also check out the giant *sugi* then.

But my father died the following day. He had met with Kanoko and her husband, and said in broken English that it was nice to meet him: "*Naisu tu mii-chuu.*" Then he compared Kanoko's pregnant belly with his own. His stomach muscles had completely withered away, and they could no longer support his internal organs. His abdomen had become swollen. That night, his condition worsened. And then on the following day, he passed away. We were all in quite a state of commotion. There was the hospital, the funeral home, the contacting of relatives, and so on. Naturally we cancelled our trip to Aso. On the way back from visiting the funeral home, the bank, and the hospital, I thought that at the very least I could bring Kanoko and her husband to visit the so-called Jakushinsan no kusu camphor tree. My father's remains were already enshrined in the funeral parlor. Oh . . . saying that makes it feel like my father is no longer my father. He had rented a space in the funeral parlor, and that's where he was now. No wait, he died, and so he wasn't really there. I mean, it wasn't the case that he either "was" there or "wasn't" there . . . This was the kind of thing that was on my mind as I was driving around.

We headed toward the rural area that runs from within Kumamoto City out to Tabaruzaka. We could see a forest of camphor trees across the way. As we got closer, it became clear that what we had thought was a forest was actually a thicket comprised of a single giant camphor tree. The tree was in a well-maintained park, but there was no one around. Flowers bloomed in clusters along the path leading from the parking lot: violets, veronica plants, henbits, tiny and common vetches. Kanoko and her husband held hands and walked around the giant camphor. I laid down on the bench that had been placed under the tree.

I looked up, looked at the tree, looked at my hands, looked at the sky. It was a lightly cloudy sky. It was a giant, giant tree covered in wrinkles. They were tired, sad hands covered in wrinkles. As I was gazing at them, I realized I'd made a big mistake. I'd just been thinking that the red color on camphor trees this time of year was from new growth. But that wasn't so. It was the old leaves that had turned red, and they were mixed in with the green of the new buds. The red leaves rustled in the wind, and rained down to cover the surface below, just like a cherry tree as it loses its blossoms.

There's one more tree I want to mention. A short while after my father died, I returned to California. I then noticed a flowering tree on the road home from my youngest daughter Tomé's school. It was one I hadn't noticed before and yet I couldn't help but feel a sense of nostalgia about it. The flowers were purple, with sharply defined, thin petals that resembled crosses. The whole tree was covered in these flowers. Under the flowers hid shiny green leaves. It was extremely beautiful, so whenever I passed by it on my bike I would slow down and admire it. Then one day I stopped my bike completely and told Tomé to go pick a few flowers and leaves off the tree. Tomé was a good girl, and so she'd do whatever embarrassing thing her mother told her to do. As I looked at the flowers and leaves that she had plucked and brought to me, I felt confident. It was a bead tree. Of the Meliaceae family, the genus *melia*, native to Asia, native to Kumamoto. Written with the Chinese character meaning "maple" or "autumn foliage" plus the character for "cedar."

Bead trees grow quickly. The ones that sprouted up about twenty years ago along the riverbed of Kumamoto's Tsuboigawa are already large trees that cast shade. They don't only grow in the wild; you can find them planted in parks here and there. In winter, their leaves fall and yellow seeds hang down on bare branches.

For a long time I'd thought this bead tree was a wax tree. You can get wax from a wax tree, and so, in feudal times, the local fiefdom in what is now Kumamoto incentivized their growth. They were planted along the old highway that ran from Ōtsu around Aso and ended up in Daibu. I remembered that long ago, when I had first moved to Kumamoto, people had told me that those trees along the highway were wax trees.

Be that as it may, the trees growing along the highway are not wax trees, they're bead trees. It was three years ago that I realized this, in the April that my mother died, in that busy time I spent traveling between California and Kumamoto during April and May. During that time, the bead trees started blooming here and there, and then they bloomed in full.

Wax trees and bead trees actually look exactly alike, but their flowers are different. The flowers of the wax tree don't draw attention. The flowers of the bead tree are gorgeously vibrant and bloom in May. And so now, these flowers that Tomé picked in our neighborhood in Southern California—these were undoubtedly from a bead tree.

If you look closely, you'll see that they are two-toned: both white and purple. Each petal on the flower is thin and sharply defined, and this is the reason why they give the impression of having a cross-like shape. But actually, they have five petals per flower bud. And they have a fragrance that commands attention. It's a powerfully sharp scent, and merely two flowers were enough to fill our whole house with its fragrance.

The bead trees over there in Kumamoto along the riverbank of the Tsuboigawa, and even the ones growing in parks over there—their flowers must be in full bloom by now. They float before my eyes. My father had also died in April, but now there was no one there anymore, and it was no longer necessary for me to return to Kumamoto throughout April and May. No me, no father, no mother. Thinking this way opened up a wide void.

I know it without having to see it. Over there along the riverbank the bead trees are being blown in the wind, and their flowers are falling off. Within the thicket along the riverbank, a male pheasant yearns for its mate, and is calling out to her. The multiflora rose is reaching maturity and splitting off into clusters, and the whole riverbank has turned white as if dusted with talcum powder.

MOUNT FUJIS AND ARBOREAL GIANTS

I set off on a journey. I left California, heading north quickly up Interstate Highway 5, which stretches across the whole state, up through the states of Oregon and Washington, and the Canadian border. I crossed the border and went to Vancouver, and then returned to America, this time heading south quickly to return home. The 4,500 kilometers I traveled, if you put it in terms of Japan, would be about the distance of leaving from Kumamoto and passing through the northwestern Hokuriku region of the main island of Honshu, and then up to Sapporo on the northern island of Hokkaido, and then following along the Pacific Ocean side of Japan back to Kumamoto.

My youngest daughter Tomé had just gotten her driver's license, and I drove the difficult roads as much as possible, but while Tomé was driving, the road changed a few times, without warning, into a mountain road with never-ending sudden curves or a downhill slope so long that you couldn't see what was coming up ahead. Each time this happened, I clenched my fists and prepared myself from the passenger's seat, thinking: "This is where I die. So it goes." On the way back, I was able to sit quietly without thinking such things, so I think Tomé had improved considerably within a span of a few days.

A few years back—no, wait, has it already been twenty years since? How quickly time passes—I took a similar trip, all by myself. I left California and headed east, crossed over the edge of the

Rocky Mountains and headed north toward the Great Plains. A friend of mine from Kumamoto had been living in Montana with her family. I stayed there a few days and then continued my journey. At one point I looked up at the sky. I saw clouds, rain, and rocks. And then I saw something dead on the road. A coyote, or maybe an opossum or a skunk or a deer was laying upside down with its feet sticking up toward the sky, and the dead bodies of its children were scattered around the dead body of their parent. The sound of the wind as it came through the opening of the car window sounded like the flute of some Indigenous tribe.

So anyway, let me get back to the story of our journey. Around this time, I had been thinking about naturalized plants. In Japan, the season for summer grasses had just begun. Along the riverbanks of Kumamoto, the young stems of *seitaka-awadachisō* (Canadian goldenrod) are surely beginning to grow all at once. *Seitaka-awadachisō* and *matsuyoigusa* (Chilean evening primrose) are both originally from North America, and I decided that I wanted to see where they grew, at their own pace, in native soil. I decided I also wanted to see some tumbleweeds while I was at it.

The real name for tumbleweed is Russian thistle. They came to America from either Russia or Ukraine at the end of the nineteenth century. They are plants, and so they grow out of the ground, but when the time comes, they leave the ground, get blown by the wind, tumble around and around, and continue to migrate while scattering their seeds. They appear often in movies that feature wandering gunmen, and while they aren't credited, they are always an important member of the cast.

I wasn't able to see any of them, however. Not the (Japanese) naturalized plants nor any tumbleweeds. The direction was wrong. We had headed north. The roads were not the least bit dry. After passing through the Central Valley that spreads throughout the center of

California (where it's hot and dry but also irrigated and fruit trees are planted in tight rows), it just got more and more damp.

And so, the first thing that caught my eye was Scotch broom. It was bright yellow, growing fresh and abundant all over the place, and in full bloom. In English, it's called "invasive." Non-native plants and animals are called "invasive" species—a word for which the nuance of the term "non-native" alone does not fit, a word which includes a vital strength and an intention to destroy natural ecosystems. But as I look at the Scotch broom, I can't help but call them invasive. I came to think perhaps they did have an evil intent to dominate over everything else and destroy the weak.

From there, what began to catch my eye upon reaching Oregon were foxgloves. This pretty flower, which can be both poisonous and medicinal, was blooming in clusters without a care as to whether they were facing sun or shade, and yet it too, of course, is invasive, having come from Europe.

And then a thicket of berries. It was climbing all over the place, like the summer kudzu in Japan, tangling things up, and growing thick and splendid. Most of it was made up of native species, maybe bramble fruit, or perhaps raspberry, or if not, then blackberry or dewberry, or swamp dewberry, but it was too early in the season. All of the clusters were in bloom and hadn't yet produced berries. I kept thinking: in a month's time I could eat all I wanted, it would be just like heaven.

Our route passed the inland area of Interstate Highway 5. It's a main thoroughfare, lacking charm and grace, but it's a steady route with many lanes where it's always easy to get gas and food. Traveling on, we passed through the Los Angeles metropolitan area, crossed over mountains, and when we exited the Central Valley, the landscape changed to grasslands and hills. We crossed a river, and then crossed a gorge. All of a sudden, on the right-hand side, there appeared a mountain that resembled Mount Fuji, covered in snow, with fields at its foot that seemed as if they had been made by a volcanic eruption some thousands of years earlier. On the left-hand side there appeared several rounded black hills that seemed to have been made by the surplus energy of the volcanic eruption. The majesty of it all took my breath away. I learned from a sign that it was called Mount Shasta, and at the hotel in Portland where we ended up that night, I looked up just what kind of history the mountain held. It was a mountain at the southern tip of the Cascade Range. The black hills were called Black Butte.

The atmosphere around the mountain was damp. Plants were flourishing; the hills and valleys were dense with them. As we entered Oregon (which was shortly after we drove past Mount Shasta), Tomé declared: "The landscape here looks like Japan. Like the countryside of Kumamoto, or when you go from Narita Airport to Haneda Airport."

There is another Mount Fuji in the Cascade Range, one that is visible from the city of Portland: Mount Hood. But there's another one to the north as well: Mount Adams. "Wow, two Mount Fujis," I think to myself, but there are even more. There's Mount St. Helens. The shape of this one changed drastically due to a volcanic eruption in the 1980s, but prior to that, it seems it was surely a Mount Fuji.

Within this damp and verdant Japan-esque landscape, all of a sudden two or three Mount Fujis appeared. It was a marvelous sight, like something out of science fiction—the kind of view that made one think maybe two or three suns or two or three moons might appear.

The Cascade Range stretches on. If you keep heading north, there's Mount Rainier, and then Mount Baker. I've heard that if you look at Mount Rainier from the coast off the city of Tacoma, it looks like the view of a snowcapped Mount Fuji from Tago Bay, as described in the ancient poem by Yamabe no Akahito. It seems long ago that people of Japanese descent used to call Mount Hood "Oregon Fuji" and Mount Rainier "Tacoma Fuji." It's a shame, but we weren't able to see the latter. Right after the Mount Fujis in Portland, the weather took a turn for the worse and it started raining. We passed by Mount Rainier again on the way home but the sky was overcast with rain clouds and we couldn't see a thing.

Rain clouds—I never see them around my house in Southern California. We're lucky if we get rain a few times a year. Someone I met in Portland made the following joke, as if they were fed up with it all: "They say it rains three hundred days out of the year around here, but that's a lie. It only rains two hundred ninety-five days. That's why there's so little green here!"

It was green there. It was so green. It was bursting with all colors of green from all kinds of grasses. There were leaves that looked like kudzu, and flowers that looked like *tora-no-o* (or "snake plant" in English). There were also leaves that looked like *fuki* (or butterbur) and leaves that looked like *takana* (or Chinese mustard). Liliaceae and Fabaceae. Ferns that were hard to distinguish outside of the fact that they were ferns. Poaceae. And then there were grasses, and there were trees. I couldn't help but stare, not knowing how to classify most of the plants, not being able to register them as anything more than a swarm of green. I couldn't help but be frustrated.

In both Oregon and Washington, I saw trees in town that I did not recognize. Frail leaves that looked as if they wouldn't make it to winter grew in abundance. These were leaves and trees that I had never seen in either Kumamoto or California. As I looked at them I thought they might be what are called *buna* (or Japanese beech) or *nire* (Japanese elm). These were names that appeared in a book that I read as I child. But I wasn't sure, so I had guessed somewhat randomly. They were delicate and refined, so different from those hackberries, oaks, and gingkoes (which I saw so many of there). I imagined that the big and strong ones were *nire*, and that the graceful, willowy ones were *buna*. Of course, there was no guarantee that they were *nire* and *buna*. At this rate, I wouldn't be able to remember their leaves by the time I returned to California.

We didn't take Highway 5 on the way back home. A number of people recommended that we not take the 5, which runs inland the whole way, but rather Highway 101, which runs along the coast. They said that the path runs right through the middle of Redwood National Park, and that it'll take more time but the scenery is amazing, and so is the ocean, and so are the trees. The Latinized scientific name for redwoods is "sequoia." Closely related to them are the Sequoiadendron—those arboreal giants that also go by the name of "giant redwoods."

I'll never forget how moved I felt when I visited Sequoia National Park for the first time a few years ago—no, wait, was this too already more than ten years ago? How quickly time passes. I had thought it would just be a regular old forest of *sugi* (or cedar trees), but as I left level ground and climbed up the mountain road, the *sugi* got progressively bigger and bigger, as if someone had cast a magic spell on them. And so in the forest, one after another, unbelievably large *sugi* came into view (the word "large" doesn't even capture how big they were). And then finally I stood before that roughly 2,000-year-old arboreal giant named "General Sherman." I felt as if my very existence had become bits and pieces. It felt as if I was prostrating myself in front of the tree.

We took Highway 101. The sea spread out, the waves drew near, the bluffs rose steeply, small islands extended outward. At times we found ourselves back inland, and then we ended up back on the coast. Whenever we went back inland, there were farmlands and there were crop fields, rivers flowed and the vegetation grew lush, and there were signs that we had never seen before that warned us to "Beware of Moose." You always see surfers and pelicans floating in the ocean in Southern California, but in this ocean, there was no one, there was nothing. Eventually, redwood forests began appearing one after another on the side of the road. Trees that were several hundreds of years old appeared one after another along the roadside, and just when we thought we had passed them by, more would appear. They continued on and on forever.

It was a real shame to just pass them by, so we pulled over to the side of the road many times to get closer to the trees. The plants growing around the large trees (which were small by comparison) were full of leaves and blooming flowers. Each one embraced the sunlight and blew in the wind, glistening. The large trees accompanied innumerable small trees. In other words, in this case, the several-hundred-year-old trees were all female. I too was female. Tomé, who I had taken along with me, was a young woman—she too was female. The young sprouts which were the trees' offspring were shorter than we were. The fresh green of these young trees, which seemed as if they were holding out their tiny hands, told me, with a determined expression that resembled the clenching of tiny teeth, that they planned to live for several hundreds of years to come.

AT WAR WITH MOLD

I have a house that I left behind in Kumamoto. It sits on the bank of a river that runs through the center of the city. It's a house that I once lived in with my family, long ago. I have been coming and going to Kumamoto frequently these past few years. And so during my comings and goings, I've been staying there. It felt cramped when I lived there with my family, but staying there all alone, it feels like too much space. It wasn't that big of a place to begin with—one big room with a loft and a lower level. If you open a door, there's one more room. The children lived up in the loft, and my husband lived with his books on the lower level. And then I lived in the room on the other side of that door.

Even now, I still live in that room. The loft is completely empty. Books remain stacked in the lower level, but what's left isn't even one percent of the amount of books that were crammed into the space long ago. Because I took the books I needed to California, and I put the books that I thought might be necessary someday later into my room, all that remained in the lower level were the forgettable books. There is also a spare bed in there, so the kid stays there when I bring her home with me. The children who had once lived in the loft have now grown up, and they no longer come back to Japan. The one I bring home with me now is the one that was born afterwards—or rather, she is the one I gave birth to after-wards. This is my house, and my father's house is close by—it only takes two or three minutes to run over there if called. For a long time, my father lived alone. My father and mother relocated from Tokyo a few years after I began living with my former husband in Kumamoto. A few years passed, and I separated from my husband. It was now my turn to relocate—this time to California. And so my father was truly all alone.

My father passed away in the middle of April. My mother had died three years prior. Of course, also in the middle of April. We didn't do any kind of formal memorial service. All I did was return to Japan for the anniversary of her death. My father's health was thoroughly declining.

No one knew whether my father was under the impression, with it being three years since her passing, that it was simply the right circumstance under which to join her, or if he was actually in decline. He died right after the anniversary of her death. It was around the time that the cherry blossoms had fallen and the paulownia trees were to bloom, and the chinquapin trees were to bloom, and the bead trees were to bloom. Along the riverbank, the multiflora roses wriggle into bloom, and the male pheasants call out incessantly for the love of the females.

Flowers arrived in rapid succession. Flower baskets and cut flowers. It got so that I lost track of who I had thanked and who I hadn't. Even now, I earnestly feel like I need to thank those I haven't already, but I guess it's probably too late.

On the day after his funeral, my cousins (who had come from Osaka) carried over some shelves from my father's house. My cousins are strong men, a few years younger than me, and they carried the shelves over easily and set them up in my house. They said, "This is good, you can put the bones on top of these, Shiromi." (Their accent made my name sound like "Shiromi" instead of "Hiromi.")

And then, just as they suggested, I lined up two urns containing bones on top of those shelves. One contained my father's, the other one contained my mother's. Since the covering of my mother's urn had turned completely yellow from sitting on top of those shelves for three years, I was given a new one by the people who worked for the company that organized my father's funeral. Two urns with brand-new coverings sat side by side on the shelves. Just to be clear, this was not my idea—it was my father's wish—or to use old-fashioned language, it was the family patriarch's final request.

He said, "Leave your mom's just like they are. When I die, put mine together with hers, and then scatter them."

And so I lined them up side by side. I put flowers in front of them. I filled the shelf with flowers. And then, leaving the shelf filled with flowers, I returned to California. There were several lilies with petals that had fallen to the ground at the time. But the majority of them were still perfectly fresh. The flowers of the bead trees and the beech trees outside the house were at their peak. Along the walls that closed in both sides of the expressway from Haneda Airport to Narita Airport, wisteria flowers bloomed on and on, as if this were their only chance to do so.

I returned to my Kumamoto home around the time that the long rainy season finally comes to an end, and the first thing that caught my eye was the large number of flower corpses.

I thought that they had probably rotted due to the humidity, but actually they had just dried out. And then they had died. I touched the dead, dried out, discolored husk of a flower, and this was enough to make it crumble. Green mold was set flying into the air.

Cut flowers look like they're dead but they're not. Sometimes if you put them in water, they'll grow roots. However, the husks of *these* flowers were completely dead. Dead flowers that appeared to be nothing but reproductive organs—truly, truly graphic. Although they dried out and turned ashen, they were graphic. A vast number of vaginas, and a vast number of penises, gorged out, all bloody, torn off and drying up just like that. To hell with sexual desire! I was confronted with the fact that they had had sex, that they were used for sex. All of this fit well with the bones of my father and mother, which sat in back within white urns covered in white cloths, and with the death that came to greet them at the end of their eighty-some-odd years of life.

Among the dried out, discolored flower husks, only the statice and the leaves of the spotted laurel still held the vibrancy of their original colors. Statice flowers are often used as a "dry flower." They seem as if they are made of paper, and they make a rustling noise. They have blue or purple calyxes attached to the tips of square stems, from which a white flower sticks out like a tongue. They grow all over Southern California. There's the planted kind that finds its way out of people's lawns, and there is also the kind that grows native near the coast. Thick leaves swirl around into a rosette pattern, and a stem stretches out above them, producing a calyx and blooming its flowers. The calyx remains forever attached to its stem, rustling all the while.

On trash day, I put the mountain of flower husks in a garbage bag. As I lifted up the flower baskets, they felt terribly light. They were so, so much heavier when they were delivered. Opening the trash bag up wide, I threw out each basket. With every little movement, green mold went flying.

The cut flowers still stood tall, arranged in a vase. I forced them into the trash bag as well. I tore off the flowers and thin stems, but the central stalks had lost all their moisture, and so I couldn't snap them in half. All I could do was bend them into a limp shape. In this way, I bent the lilies. I bent the roses. Chrysanthemums, lilies, and even more roses—I bent them all. The bird-of-paradise flowers indeed looked like birds. It felt like I was bending the corpses of birds that had their mouths open.

There was a centipede corpse in the sink drain. This was a house where centipedes often made appearances, and I've killed living ones many times. Centipedes are strong, and they just don't seem to die no matter how many times you whack them. You whack them but it doesn't crush them or tear them apart. They must have a structure in which there is no space between their flesh and their shell.

The one in the sink was all limp like boiled noodles, with a fresh green color about it. I hadn't noticed it the night before. Perhaps it had died a long time ago and dried up, its color fading. The reason I didn't notice it the night before was because it didn't have this green color then. I let the water run freely without noticing it. Had it soaked up the water and started to swell, just like dried seaweed or dried gourd, and returned to its original color? It wasn't pleasant. I nervously picked it up with chopsticks, and then washed it down the drain. It must be all swollen up by now, somewhere in the pitch-black darkness.

Every year, I get worried about mold in the summertime. It's summer half the year in Kumamoto, and so it smells moldy for half of the year. The other half of the year is not as bad as the summertime, but it still smells moldy.

Once long ago, someone who came to visit said to me: "Hiromi, you lit some incense, didn't you?" But I wasn't doing it for the sake of the fragrance. Because it is the only way to get rid of the smell of mold, I had bought some cheap incense at a general store that carried Asian goods, and I was burning it nonstop. The stuff I bought had names that resembled bath salts, like "Jasmine" and "Eucalyptus."

I had once received some incense that I was told was a souvenir from the Buddhist temple at Mount Koya. It had an expensive-smelling fragrance that was far nobler than that of jasmine or eucalyptus. However, when I lit it, I found that it was wrapped up in too many memories: before this incense was ever used as an anti-mold countermeasure or to create an "Asian atmosphere," it held a central position in esoteric Buddhism, as well as at temples, in Buddhist memorial services and rites for the dead . . . Well now, that wouldn't work. In order to fight back in the war against mold, I needed to stay grounded and go on living my everyday life.

I was here last year right before the rainy season. My father was still alive then. I felt his intense gaze clinging to me, and I left his house, saying: "OK, I'll be back in July." I figured it would surely get damp once the rains started, and that it would be good to get some air circulating, if only a little bit, so I cracked the windows in my own house before leaving. And then I did not return for the entirety of the rainy season. When I did return after the rainy season had ended, my house (where no one was living) was covered in mold. I had never seen anywhere so moldy before. The window frames were bright white, the books and bookshelves in the lower level were pure black. Every year I had complained: "It smells moldy! It smells moldy!" But I hardly ever came across any mold that you could actually see with your own eyes. And so I began training in non-incense-based anti-mold countermeasures. I bought a dehumidifier. I used a ventilating fan. I left that fan running nonstop. And then this year arrived. At the end of the rainy season, we had a huge rainfall. It was a record-breaking rainfall that fell throughout the island of Kyushu, including in Kumamoto. Mountains crumbled, rivers overflowed, people died.

A neighbor told me: "It just kept raining like I've never seen it rain before. It rained as if the sky had split open and dumped giant buckets of water down. Rain clouds just kept coming and going from the East China Sea and the West China Sea."

Another neighbor told me: "About every twenty years or so we get huge rainfalls that flood the city. Over these past ten-odd years, flood management in Kumamoto has been pretty much under control. Right around here they created a pond meant to prevent flooding. That helped. If it had been twenty years ago, we'd have been flooded."

This year, the minute I opened the front door to my house, there was a strong odor—stronger than the usual smell the house has in summer. I wondered if this was what dead bodies smelled like. I wondered this because the minute I opened the door, what came flying into view were two urns side sitting side by side, and a mountain of withered, oh so withered, flower husks. Come to think of it, the smell of dead bodies is not the smell of death itself, it's the smell of life having lived and died, and the decomposition thereof.

Mold spreads from things that have been touched by human hands. My father's leather wallet had been sitting the whole time on top of a table. That got moldy. The cutting board and kitchen knives got moldy. Chopsticks and dishcloths, the chocolate I had started eating and then left behind—all moldy. The area around the kitchen sink and the beds—all moldy. As I picked things up, mold moved freely within the space between the object and the skin of my hand. Even on the soles of my feet, mold moved freely.

I wondered whether or not naturalized plants were growing in profusion along the riverbank, but it was still too early. I think they were all weeded out before the rains, and they hadn't grown back. I couldn't find any plants that had been withered in the heavy rains. The riverbank had an expression that resembled exhaustion, due to the fact that the roots of the various grasses that grew there were still the color of mud. The kudzu and the young sprouts of *seita-ka-awadachisō* (Canadian goldenrod), the *yabugarashi* (bushkiller) and *kanamugura* (wild hops), the *seibanmorokoshi* (Johnson grass), which had been weeded out but had started growing back—the roots of each were still mud colored. The bead tree had leaves so lush that I couldn't tell what was what, with its fruit growing in tight clumps. Kudzu and other vines were creeping up to the tops of the trees, trying to flourish even more than they already were.

SUMMER GRASS

It's late summer. On the riverbanks of Kumamoto, summer grass must be growing like crazy, as if it's its last chance to do so. It must be thriving, growing quick and tall. It must be blooming flowers, sprouting out bulbs, swaying in the wind. It's a shame, I'm here in California at the moment, so I can't see that magnificent scene. It's a real, real shame.

Allow me to give a brief introduction. The plants that grow along the riverbanks of Kumamoto are mostly of the Asteraceae family, the Poaceae family, and the Fabaceae family, and except for the kudzu and silver grass, they are all naturalized plants.

Summer grass—a phrase used in that famous poem from the late seventeenth century by Matsuo Bashō: "Summer grass—all that remains of warriors' dreams."[1] For a long time, I had thought "summer grass" referred to large clumps of *seitaka-awadachisō* (*Solidago altissima*) or *ō-arechinogiku* (*Conyza sumatrensis*). I thought, "It's gotta be them, those symbols of life that grow out of and prosper on top of those that have already fallen into ruin and have faded away." But that wasn't the case. It would be one thing if they were plants that had come to Japan in the very distant past, but *seitaka-awadachisō* and *ō-arechinogiku* both arrived after the Meiji Restoration and couldn't have proliferated among the remains of warriors' dreams in the middle of the Edo period. It must have been an entirely different landscape all together.

I've loved weeds ever since I was child. I grew up on the back
streets of a poor neighborhood in Tokyo, reading Ernest Thompson
Seton and *The Jungle Book*. I longed for nature, but the air around
me was polluted, and everything there gasped for breath: the city,
the river, all the living things, and all those things that we ate, as
well. As far as nature goes, weeds were about all I had. And so, as I
walked around, I looked down toward the weeds. I learned the term
"naturalized plant" from a field guide that I used to look things up
that I saw along the sides of the roads. And then I realized how
each and every weed I saw was a naturalized plant. And how the
majority of them were alike—they were native to North America.

Even though I was child, I was well acquainted with the idea of
things being native to North America. That's because the animals
that appear in Seton's *Wild Animals I Have Known* are mostly
ones that are native to North America: coyotes, wolves, wild boars,
ruffled grouses, bighorn sheep. Each one is strong, smart, they live,
they die. Children everywhere, as young as ten years old, learned
that this is what it meant, at a fundamental level, to behave as a
living thing. And so I had thought that plants like *himemukashiyo-
mogi* (*Erigeron canadensis*), *seitaka-awadachisō* (*Solidago altissima*),
butakusa (*Ambrosia artemisiifolia*), *himejo-on* (*Erigeron annuus*),
and *harushi-on* (*Erigeron philadelphicus*)—and no, not just these
weeds of the Asteraceae family, but also *matsuyoigusa* (*Oenothera
stricta*) of the Onagraceae family, and *amerika-fūro* (*Geranium car-
olinianum*) of the Geranianceae family, too—these must all stick
to the fundamentals of living things as well: getting strong, getting
smart, living, and then dying.

This, you see, was North America.

When I came to North America, I saw that the people here
were overweight and that the food was no good. The only native
coyotes you see are corpses on the road. The plants that had been
naturalized into Japan were nowhere to be found. I had thought

that they would be flourishing in their native home, to an extent that far surpassed their success in Japan, but one can't observe what isn't there.

At the end of October, the riverbanks of Kumamoto are dyed a bright yellow by *seitaka-awadachisō*. These get entangled with the native *susuki* (or Japanese pampas grass), which is pure white. Bright yellow and pure white—how very splendid!

You can't find a single *seitaka-awadachisō* plant in the area around San Diego in Southern California. You can find grasses that resemble *himemukashiyomogi* or *himejo-on*, but not only do they have different shapes, they don't have that same kind of brazenness that the ones in Japan have. The ones here feel balanced, living calmly in their corner of society, and seeming as if they would never miss a neighborhood association meeting. Is that because this is their natural habitat?

The ocean is nearby, and there are lagoons here and there. There are also special plants that only grow along the coast and along the beach. Nature is protected in these areas. Along the roads near these preservations, I saw some weak-looking *matsuyoigusa* (or Evening primrose in English). They were most prevalent in early summer. Two or three of them were lined up and in bloom. Now that it's turned to autumn, there are none left. But I found one the other day. It wasn't near a lagoon, but in an empty lot nearby. I stopped my car and took a close look. A little over one meter in height, its roots formed a rosette shape with several stems growing out. Yellow flowers were blooming on the ends on the stems. The flowers on it that had withered were red. I picked some, brought them home, and put them in a vase, and two of the flowers opened up overnight. Flowers with soft petals that were an almost transparent yellow opened up.

I have a book called *San Diego County Native Plants*. It's a book I bought here at a local botanical garden. It seems like it was

self-published, and for this reason it conveys the enthusiasm of
the people who wrote it. It's actually very exhaustive, and you can
find anything in it. And so I found out that this flower was marsh
matsuyoigusa, or marsh primrose in English.

The spot where I found marsh primrose in early summer is now
covered in tall grasses of the Asteraceae family. They seem like
himemukashiyomogi, but made heavier, with leaves that are stiff
and round, and stems that move in close, blooming fresh yellow
flowers on their tips.

I looked it up in my book: golden aster, of the Asteraceae family.
But it's not an aster. Its Latin name is *Heterotheca*. It's a plant that
hasn't come to Japan, and one that seems like it has no intention
of doing so, and because of that I wondered if it even made sense
to give a Japanese name to every single plant, but then I looked it
up online and the Japanese name is *arechi-oguruma*.

Of course the word *arechi*, or "wasteland," is attached to the name.
It grows in a place that is dried up and wasted, and the sight of
this tall grass clumping together and blowing in the wind is truly
brutal, as it appears to narrate the hardships of naturalized plants.
But it's a native plant. Even if it isn't a naturalized plant, and even
if it does grow native here, the fact that there are native plants like
this that live such hard lives—it brought me some relief. And so
I thought: if these plants were like people and had free will and
money enough to buy a plane ticket, they would probably up and
leave their native land behind.

In any case, it's dry here. It's a desert-like climate, but because
it's near the ocean, everything is salty. The marsh where the marsh
primroses grow is actually part of a lagoon, and the water there is
saltwater. Seaside plants grow near the beach: ice plant, *okahijiki*
(*Salsola komarovii*), common reeds and cattails. It's cloudy in the
morning and it clears up in the afternoon. In the evening, the wind

blows in from the sea. If you go about twenty minutes inland, the saltiness gives way to a sandiness, and everything dries up.

People always say that the weather in Southern California is so good, but that's only true of the temperature. There's not enough rain here. Nowhere near enough. And so all of the native plants have narrow leaves. They get heavy and grow fur. As someone who knows that the vines grow every which way on the riverbanks of Kumamoto, and that plants like kudzu flourish while dropping large and tender green leaves, it seems to me that the plants here live their lives with scowling faces and gritted teeth.

I've dreamt about it many times—what would happen if I uprooted the plants from here and transplanted them to Kumamoto? Brought to a place with such a high temperature, one that was also so humid, with a lot of rainfall, a place where it was easy to live and reproduce, the transplanted plants would be shocked; they would rejoice; they would grow and spread in rapid succession; they would annihilate the meek native plants. The plants that grow here in California, like sage (there are many varieties, and they're all tenacious) and golden aster (*Heterotheca*), would form giant communities and rustle in the winds of Kumamoto, just like the now-naturalized *matsuyoigusa* and *ō-arechinogiku* did long ago. And then, they would be seen as invasive species, as plants with bad intentions, and they would be exterminated. . . . In other words, it would not be a good idea to transplant them.

I want to talk some more about *matsuyoigusa*.

The plants of the genus *matsuyoigusa* (*Oenothera* in English) that have made their way to Japan are mostly of North American origin, and it seems that there are many that come from the area where I live in Southern California. *Ō-matsuyoigusa*, with its big flowers, used to be common in the past, but has now become scarce, and I've heard that *me-matsuyoigusa* and *arechi-matsuyoigusa* look so much alike that one cannot tell them apart. It seems *ko-matsuyoigusa* creeps along the ground like a vine. And to be precise about things, they say *tsukimisō* (*Oenothera tetraptera*) is different from common *matsuyoigusa*. It seems the famous author Dazai Osamu got it wrong when he wrote about *tsukimisō* growing on Mount Fuji.

I don't know which variety, if it was *ō-*, or *me-*, or *arechi-*, but when I was a child, I found *matsuyoigusa* all over the place. All of my family that lived in the backstreets of Tokyo mistakenly called *tsukimisō* "*matsuyoigusa*." As a child, I thought that *matsuyoigusa* (written in phonetic katakana characters) was the official name for *tsukimisō* (written in Chinese characters), just like how there are two names for cumulonimbus clouds: *nyūdōgumo* (written in Chinese characters) and the official name *sekiranun* (written in katakana).

Speaking of *tsukimisō*, there is a plant called *hiru-tsukimisō* (*Oenothera speciosa*) that is of Mexican origin (the English common name is "Mexican primrose"). In Kumamoto, it escaped from a garden and turned feral. It has an ephemeral, pretty pink color. When it first caught my eye, I doubted what I saw. I puzzled over how in the world a *matsuyoigusa* had turned such a color, how had it gotten so short, how it was in bloom at that time of year. It took a while for me to realize it was a different grass of the same family and same genus. Even here in California, it's a popular garden plant, so I tried planting some in our garden, where everything wilts right away. Since Mexico is so close by (only thirty minutes by car), I figured it was like transplanting something into a neighbor's garden, but it withered without taking root. Perhaps I can only grow something like *ō-kinkeigiku* ("lanceleaf tickseed" in English) in my garden. It's a plant that has become a problem in Japan, but it's native to America, so it won't cause anyone any trouble here.

There is a park next door to our house that has become a wasteland, and I've written many times about how the native plants there are protected. In spring, the flowers bloom. Lots of different flowers bloom. But the ones that bloom the most, and bloom the earliest, and stay in bloom the longest, are related to the genus *matsuyoigusa* or *Oenothera*, within the Onagraceae family.

They bloom yellow flowers. There are four petals on each flower. The flowers turn red as they wither. There are also ones that don't turn red. There are also some that have stems that stand upright. There are some that form a rosette shape and creep about. Although they are plants that one cannot find in Japan, when you see one suddenly, you think: "Ah! It's *matsuyoigusa*!" They bloom throughout spring, and stay through summer, but then disappear completely around the end of the season. When I looked them up in my book, they were in the genus *Camissonia*. They used to be in the genus *matsuyoigusa* long ago, but it seems they were separated for various reasons. That's why they look so similar. They appear to be *matsuyoigusa* at first glance, but then you change your mind, realizing that they're too small, or that they're standing upright, or that they're creeping along the ground.

Even in that park next door to our house, non-native plants find their way in. Since the park is designed to protect native species, the non-native plants are, of course, forcibly exterminated. One that's seen as particularly hostile is ice plant, which was planted as ground cover, and holds water in its leaves and grows easily, spreading out all over, covering everything up, destroying everything in its path. Sometimes the organization that manages the park conducts a large-scale assault on the ice plant, and the corpses that have been uprooted are piled up in heaps. I know they're plants, but there is no other word I can use besides "corpses." It's a terrible sight, and I have to cover my eyes.

Ice plant. Considering that I've introduced all the other plants by their real names, it wouldn't be right to use such a random name for this plant only. It's related to plants like *tsuruna* (*Tetragonia tetrag-*

onioides) and *matsubagiku* (*Lampranthus spectabilis*), and belongs
to the family Aizoaceae. The type that is truly seen as an enemy
around here is the variety called *Carpobrotus edulis*, which is native
to South Africa. It blooms flowers that look like big, wide-open
eyes. They are either whitish-yellow or fresh pink in color. Among
the piled up, uprooted stems and leaves, the flowers lay dead, their
eyes still open. The colors of the dead flowers fade away. It's a truly
terrible sight, and I have to cover my eyes.

A landscape in which naturalized plants gave off a rumbling
sound, and grew thick and abundant along the riverbanks and road-
sides—that was my home. By no means was it a landscape where
the setting sun fades into a field of flowers, as the old song goes.
Even though I've learned that naturalized plants have exterminated
the native plants, I've come on over to the side of the invasive, and
resigned myself, thinking, "Hmm, well, the native plants were weak,
and so it goes." If anything, naturalized plants are the ones that are
fierce and indefatigable, and, to an extent, it seems that they have
served as my role models.

I had thought this landscape would continue on forever. But
it didn't. Naturalized plants change. Again and again, they get
replaced by those much stronger than themselves. *Matsuyoigusa*,
which naturalized to Japan and grew so abundantly there, is now
hard to come by. It's the story of bright yellow *seitaka-awadachisō*—
its vital energy in decline. It's the story of bright white *susuki*—its
strength coming back.

WHY I KILLED THE PAMPAS GRASS

When I was about eighteen or nineteen years old, I learned that the Japanese sound "*ho*," with its single syllable, expresses the following: "to appear outside" and "to stand out or tower above." This same "*ho*," employing both meanings, appears in the term "*kuni no mahoroba*," an ancient poetic phrase used to refer to the capital of Nara, once considered the best place to live in the country, as well as in the word "*ho*", meaning the ear or head of a plant. It was a moving experience to discover all of this. The heads of plants ("*ho*"), and particularly the heads of plants of the fountain grass or foxtail variety, closely resemble the fluffy tails of puppies, or kitties, or bunnies—to an extent that you almost can't believe they are plants. I wondered if the "*po*" in the word for tail ("*shippo*") was originally pronounced "*ho*" and perhaps once carried the same kind of meaning.

Right now in Southern California, the heads of grasses in the Poaceae family are blowing in the wind, as if it were autumn.

Autumn holds a special place in American culture—more so than spring or summer or winter. They spend so much time searching for that autumn feeling, first with Halloween at the end of October and then Thanksgiving right after it, that you get the impression that a full year's worth of seasonal feeling gets used up in the pursuit. And because the traditional image of that autumn-ness belongs to the America of the East Coast, it doesn't match the climate of Southern California.

In any case, here the sunlight is strong and flowers bloom one after another all year long. But the days get shorter. The sunset comes earlier. And with that you get the feeling that it's become autumn. And then you notice, huh, there sure are a lot of Poaceae grasses within the landscaping around town, aren't there? They're planted in the lawns around office buildings and in the communal areas around apartment buildings. You can find large quantities of them in gardening shops as well. What these grasses express is the joy of the harvest. I think this must be an ancestral memory, recalling the history of America.

When I was a child, I had called the Poaceae family (which is now called "*ine-ka*" in Japanese, which literally means "rice family") by the old word for it: "*kahon-ka*." I liked the sound of that word. The word *kahon-ka* always accompanied the word "naturalized plant." That's because most of the naturalized plants I came across were of the Poaceae family, or *kahon-ka*. Actually, no, that wasn't all. I thought it was a cool word because I didn't know what it meant. When I looked it up, it said the first "*ka*" means "the shape of a rice plant" or "the shape of a drooping head of rice." The "*hon*," it said, "represents the roots of a tree." All things must pass, and I am now fully accustomed to using the new name, "*ine-ka*."

We say "*ine-ka*," but within this "rice family" is also bamboo, wheat, pampas grass, and flatsedge. In English, the common name for this family is the Grass family. In Latin, it's either Poaceae or Gramineae. "Poa" apparently means "grass" in Ancient Greek, and "Gramen" means "grass" or "covered in grass" in Latin. I wonder—when it comes to the various Eastern languages, perhaps people were fascinated by the plant that gave them rice to eat, and when it comes to the various Western languages, maybe people were more interested in the grasses of the prairies that bent in the wind.

Now, in the fields of Southern California, pampas grasses of the *ine-ka* or Poaceae family are rustling in the wind.

At first glance they appear to have heads like those of *susuki* (*Miscanthus sinensis*), but the root stocks are giant, and the heads are giant, and everything about them is giant. They have fluffy heads that have a silver color with some cream mixed in. The Japanese name for this plant is *shiroganeyoshi*, and while they belong to the *ine-ka* or Poaceae family, it seems they don't belong to the genus *Miscanthus* (which is *susuki* in Japanese) and are native to the Pampa lowlands of South America. If so, it would have been better to call it *pampa-kusa* (with *kusa* meaning "grass") in Japanese, rather than transliterate the English name, which is how it's currently done.

If the way *susuki* sprouts its head and then rustles in the wind can be likened to the way human men release pheromones in a display of their masculinity, then pampas grass can be compared to a more elegant image—that of a silverback gorilla leading a pack of females in the face of a strong gale.

Many years ago, right around this time of year, I got to ride in a hot-air balloon. From an empty lot near the coast we ascended into the sky, were blown by the ocean wind, and drifted inland. Below us, I could see housing developments that were under construction and spacious agricultural plantations, as well as empty lots that seemed to have been left behind. Pampas grass grew here and there in those empty lots. I didn't know at the time that pampas grass was a naturalized plant. I also didn't know it was considered an invasive species. All I knew was that I was captivated by its stunning beauty as it stood out in white in the midst of the dusk down below.

As we started to descend and got closer to the ground, I saw that they were much taller in height than humans, that the size of their root stocks exceeded what one could carry in one's arms, that their silver heads and their leaves that seemed to rise up and flow down in heaps held an overwhelmingly assertive strength.

And so I fell in love with pampas grass. Every day, I thought only of pampas grass, and through the power of my thoughts, suddenly some appeared in our yard. It grew, heads appeared, and they rustled in the wind. I was happy that the pampas grass was growing, and I told everyone: "That house that's growing the pampas grass in the front yard, that's my place."

But while I gazed out at the pampas grass over the course of many years, I began to feel as if it was getting out of control. Little by little, a feeling like neglect arose within my heart. Little by little, I began to think it might be better if there was no pampas grass, and then, little by little, I regretted planting it. That thought grew in size, just like the plants themselves grew, and then finally, it was time.

A gardener comes every other week. I say "gardener," but his main job is to gather up the eucalyptus leaves that fall all over the yard using a leaf blower. He doesn't understand my interest in gardening at all, and sometimes he trims the geranium bushes down so much that they look like the back of someone's head with a crew cut. He relentlessly pulls up the weeds that I so painstakingly transplanted there. I got the sense that he thought as little of the pampas grass that I had started growing as he did of the free-growing geranium or the small weeds.

He told me repeatedly: "You should pull them out." I was told: "If you wait, they'll get out of hand." Each time, I would hold off, thinking that they looked so much like plants in Japan that they made me feel nostalgic, and so I wanted to wait to pull them up.

One day I confessed to the gardener that I wanted them removed. As an expression that read "I told you so" came over his face, he thought it over. If it were a couple of years ago, back when he had wanted to pull them up, he could have done so easily. But now the roots had grown too large.

He went back to his car to look for his machete, and then used it to cut away at the roots vigorously. He then used a hoe to slash into them. Before long, the roots were reduced to shreds. And so he began removing the rootstocks from the yard little by little. I didn't think it was a job that could be finished in one day's time. The roots were too big. But it was over before I knew it. After a few hours had passed, a large, gaping hole had been opened up.

There are three palm trees growing in my front yard. Because they were planted when the house was built, they're probably around fifty years old. I myself planted the rosemary and the geranium bushes. Enduring the droughts and water shortages, they've grown rampant without hesitation. There is also some guara, which belongs to the Onagraceae family, that I transplanted. It grows wild around here, so I had picked some up from the side of the road. Within the space occupied by these plants, the pampas grass grew fierce. It got to the point where it was trying to squeeze out all the other plants. Now it had become a gaping absence.

Many years passed.

Now it's that time of year again when the silver heads of the pampas grass sway in the wind, and I wonder as I watch it: Why did I kill it? I can't remember the reason. All I can remember is how, little by little, it got out of control, and how, little by little, I lost affection for it.

It wasn't my first time killing a plant. No matter how many times you kill plants, they come back to life. I get the feeling that even if I kill a certain plant here, it'll become a different plant somewhere else. The way of life for plants is in no way like ours, where individuals are individuals and death is death, and where the death of an individual means the absolute end. This made it easy to kill plants without concern. I gave up on plants that had become shabby-looking or plants that were sick and cut them off at their roots. But it was my first time killing a plant in that manner—going so far as to ask someone else for help in cutting apart and removing a large plant that was in no way weak.

I went on a run around my neighborhood, searching for the reason why I had killed it. I thought I should a take careful look at some pampas grass. It almost felt like I was on a hunt. And then I found my prey in the spot where I thought it would be.

There was none to be found in any residential areas. There was also none growing in the rocky soil where human hands couldn't reach. Where it did grow was in spots next to the residential areas that remained out of reach for humans. Outside the plot of land to the rear of the houses. The entrance to the highway. The highway median. The empty lots marked for home construction. And the roadsides that didn't face people's homes.

Each shining silver head of pampas grass was fluffy enough to fill a pillow. Touching them, they felt as smooth as silk. They puffed up in the wind, were blown about in the wind, and swayed madly. And I saw that within those silver heads there were many old heads mixed in, withering as they stood there. It slowly dawned on me why I had killed the pampas grass.

The old heads lose their color, their flowers and seeds fall off, and they start balding. They end up merely clinging to the tips of gangly grass. The length of their stalks stands out and seems extra long, even though they are no different in length from the ones with new heads on them. The old heads don't end up hidden within the new ones.

That's right. For the first few years, our pampas grass shined silver with new heads, but eventually became a mix of living and dead husks. And then, with each passing year, the dead ones came to stand out. The dead husks, you could say, stood straight up in a dreadful manner, like scarecrows or ghosts.

In my backyard. The first thing I would see there when I returned home was this dreadful sight. Leaving the house and coming back home was, for me, a regular, everyday occurrence. Shopping, picking up the kids, taking the dogs for a walk. Even though this was the case, whenever I returned home, I got the feeling I had returned to a wasteland. The wind blew through it. I had prepared myself for an unceremonious death, but it felt like I was being made to reaffirm this repeatedly.

A few years passed. In the gaping hole in my front yard, two varieties of grass had, once again, spouted out, each looking healthy. They're swaying in the wind now.

One of them belongs to the genus *Pennisetum*. Cultivated varieties of this genus are popular for gardening. There are all different kinds, but the one you see most often (which is also the one growing in my yard) is brown with some purple mixed in, and it looks like a giant green foxtail. The head is lovely and fluffy and seems warm, as if it were radiating its own body heat. It's hard to believe it's a plant. It fully ripens this time of year, and if you stroke the head, seeds come rustling off. And then they take off running from the yard.

The other one is a genuine *susuki* (or *Miscanthus*). The Japanese *susuki* has a very bad reputation in North America. In terms of naturalized plants in Japan, they are similar to the lanceleaf coreopsis, which is of North American origin and was introduced into Japan as a garden plant but has now become hated as an invasive species. But in spite of this, even now you can find several varieties of *susuki* for sale at gardening stores over here, and because they sell them, people buy them—I mean, it's really none of my business, so please excuse me. The *susuki*, too, forms a head and scatters in the wind, taking off out of the yard. The one that found its way to my yard also took off from somewhere and set out. Seeking refuge, it was overjoyed to find the yard of someone from Japan. I want to say to it: "It must've been rough being where you were until now. It must've been lonely. You must've missed white rice and miso soup." Full of these feelings, I will try to take good care of it.

I visited several different places in the middle of autumn.

I was at home in California until the end of September. From there I went to Japan and visited Tokyo and Kumamoto. While shuttling back and forth between them in the middle of October, I went to Narita Airport, and flew from there to Oslo. Then from Oslo I made a connection somewhere and returned home to California at the end of October. It was autumn everywhere I went. Each place had its own respective autumn.

A strong heat wave continued throughout September in California. Everyone said it was "so hot, unusually hot." I had heard my Japanese friends and acquaintances complaining bitterly about the heat over there, and so I resigned myself to thinking: "This is it?" Here in Southern California, they haven't experienced the effects of global warming enough yet. Go ahead, take a look at Kumamoto—every year the temperature rises, and they have to revise the record of how many days the temperature rises above thirty degrees Celsius. Rainfall, which has always been heavy there, gets even more extreme each year. This summer Kumamoto was assaulted by a rainfall they called "unprecedented in recorded history." Compared to that, the weather in Southern California is always gentle. No matter how hot it gets, it doesn't last but a few weeks, and the humidity is low. They've never experienced the kind of heat you get in a Japanese summer. The kind of heat where you are plastered in sweat and it feels like you're being fried like tempura, like oil is meticulously pouring out of every pore, one by one—they've never experienced *that* kind of heat before. But what goes around comes around, and there's nothing wrong with that.

Around this time of year, the fruit of the southern magnolia tree catches one's eye. The fruit, which resembles a small pineapple, grows in abundance toward the top of the tree. It matures at the end of September, and comes sprouting out bright red. It's a red like you wouldn't believe.

There are many plants in Southern California that produce red fruit. Nandias, firethorns, rowans—these all grow them. Each one produces sparkling red fruit that look like fish roe. It's a red that makes you want to pluck the fruit off the tree and hold it in your hand. But nothing matches the red of the fruit that grows on the southern magnolia. It's such a deep red that it looks black. No wait, red is red. It's the kind of red that feels evil. Because it's close to the color that bursts forth as you slice open flesh, it feels as if it is a condensed form of the very craving itself that one gets for meat.

Southern magnolias are often large trees with flowers that bloom and fruit that grows up toward the top end. The flowers are an endlessly noble white. Because it produces such a vulgar fruit, I . . . No, actually, it's because it produces such a vulgar fruit *while also having* a certain nobility that I feel a true affinity for this tree.

I looked it up, and southern magnolias are native to the United States, specifically the southeast part of country, which is not where California is. Its leaves are thick, and shiny enough to reflect light. They seem to be a type of laurel tree. They are not suited to the climate and natural conditions here. This is the kind of place where the saltiness of the sea meets the desert climate, where the leaves of plants are thin and narrow, or have furry surfaces. (I mean, of course there are some exceptions, but overall . . .) As I look up at the fruit of the southern magnolia, which is of a totally different nature, whose very existence here is bizarre—gazing at this oddity, I forget for a moment just what in the world it is that I'm looking at. Then I realize: oh right, it's a leaf covered in fur. But was I wrong? Was it an illusion? I myself was not native to the glossy-leaved evergreen forest region of Kumamoto, but rather to an industrial zone on the loamy layer of the Kantō plain where Tokyo is located—a place where no woods or forests were left standing.

Resigning myself to the endlessly cruel summer heat that lingered on into late September, I headed to Kumamoto. However, I found in the heat a certain unexpected honesty. In two or three days after arriving in Kumamoto, I became aware of the scent of osmanthus.

The first thing I discovered after moving from Tokyo to Kumamoto was that Kumamoto does not have four seasons. But people from Kumamoto would dislike my saying so. It is a thing of pride for those who have lived within Japanese culture to say that there are four seasons here. To tell them there are not four seasons is the same as saying "this is not your home." It feels as if you are looking down on them. Not wanting to hurt anyone's feelings, I wouldn't say it out loud, but year after year, global warming has made it known. We have reached the limit of pretending that we still believe in four seasons. And now that I, myself, have been steeped in the waters of Kumamoto, why should I hesitate to say so?

I'll say it clearly. In short: when summer arrives in Kumamoto, a steady, intense heat lingers on. An intense heat that makes you ready to quit being human and become a reptile or insect instead. Reptiles and insects live on without hardship, but mammals and plants get exhausted. While trees and grass may be exhausted, they are at least able to keep growing because of the humidity. But it is this humidity that makes it so unbearably cruel to humans.

There are Japanese horse chestnut trees planted in a park nearby. In the summer, they suffer from the heat and their leaves frizzle up. It's a shame. They shouldn't have planted them and instead have

planted something like bead trees or camphor trees. But humans
do unreasonable things. The horse chestnuts are quite admirable
though, as no matter how burnt their leaves get, they produce nuts
and drop them when the season arrives. The nuts are a shiny light
brown in color and are the exact same shape and color as the chest-
nuts that fall along the roads in Europe—the ones we call *maronie*
or *kashitan* in Japanese. I collect some every year, but I have never
once tried eating one. To eat them you have to cover them in lye and
then wash them off. The whole process is quite an ordeal. Sitting
uneaten, at some point they dry out and lose their luster.

But no matter what the heat in Kumamoto is like, nothing can
overcome our larger fate—the one tied to the sun and the rotation
of the planet. Things soften as October arrives and ushers in its own
kind of heat. It feels the way Tokyo did in the middle of summer
when I was a child. It stays like that for a while and feels increas-
ingly cool and fresh. Lots of people walk around town dressed in
autumn clothing. But even if it feels like autumn, the temperature
just doesn't want to drop, and it remains harsh in actuality.

Then the temperature drops a little bit. It's meant to get quite
cold (household heaters serve as proof of this), but now that it's
autumn and I have endured the trauma inflicted by summer, I'm
not able to recall how it's really supposed to feel.

It's around that time that flowers start to bloom. Like the sa-
sanqua and the camellia. They reach their peak. One after another,
they reach their peak.

In Kumamoto there is a common type of flower cultivation called
Higo rokka, which is named after the Higo samurai clan. The *rokka*
or "six flowers" are camellia, sasanqua, morning glory, peony, chry-
santhemum, and iris. Here and there you find large camellia and
sasanqua trees. Flowers bloom on these large trees like it's their
last chance to do so. The blooming season is long and continues
up until around April. The season ends long after the cherry trees

have already lost their flowers, right around a special day: *Hachijū hachiya* or the eighty-eighth night after the beginning of spring on the lunar calendar. Or least that has been my impression these past few years. In Kumamoto, it's an autumn you cannot truly call "autumn," and a winter you cannot truly call "winter."

A few years ago, however, I witnessed a real autumn. I saw it clearly. In mid-August I pushed my way into the thickets of Mount Aso. It's hard to forget the beauty of the autumn flowers I came across. Aso is, by nature, a cool enough place to not need air conditioning. In the fields, flowers grow in profusion: bush clover, pinks, golden lace, globe thistles, and pampas grass. I recalled the memories of my ancestors, for whom this profusion signaled the arrival of autumn. The ancient days of the poetry collection *Man'yōshu* and *The Tale of Genji*, and even further back. They must have been alive at that time, my ancestors' ancestors' ancestors, and their ancestors as well. While life loomed over them, while they lived and died, they saw them: these flowers of autumn.

Osmanthus wafted gently through the air at first. It got stronger with each day, and lodged in my nasal cavity, and got into every nook and cranny of every fold in my brain. It got to the point where it was all I could think about, whether awake or asleep. It ceased to be merely a scent or fragrance, and I began to think of it as a foul odor.

The *susuki* was in full bloom along the riverbank. Ten years or so ago the riverbank must have been even more steeped in bright yellow from the *seitaka-awadachisō*. The way it was now, it had lost much of its strength and it grew in small clusters. It was losing out to the *susuki*. To rise and to fall—this seems to be one fate for naturalized plants and invasive species.

What I called *susuki* was probably *ogi* (silvergrass). It covers the parts of the riverbank that are inaccessible to humans. From the way it spreads out all over, and from the whiteness of its puffy tips,

I get the sense that it is *ogi* rather than *susuki*. But I can't be sure, as I am just a novice who only saw it from a distance.

One day I saw something terrible. It happened as I got on the Kyushu Expressway from the Tosu Interchange and headed towards Kumamoto. *Susuki* was swaying gently off the shoulder of the highway. It was *susuki* and definitely not *ogi*. I knew this because there were dense clumps of it rising up. I sped right by it, and the landscape flowed past me, and so I wasn't able to get a close look. But before long something unbelievable happened with the *susuki*, and I was able to make out what was going on. Believe it or not there was pampas grass growing. Just like *susuki*, it had been planted along the shoulder of the highway. Pampas grass stood in large clusters one after the other along the shoulder. Standing there, their silver tips blew noisily in the wind. As they blew about, they shed countless seeds. They, themselves, had ridden the wind and scattered to this very spot.

This is how invasive species take off and come to invade another territory. What were the people who planted it thinking? Were they only thinking about cars? Did they think about the environment? In a few years, when this will definitely become a problem, when it becomes a disaster, the amount of *susuki* will decrease remarkably, and the pampas grass will conquer the land. Certain invasive species, however, get singled out, and the dead remains of uprooted pampas grass will then lay in heaps. As I imagined this scenario, I sped down the Kyushu Expressway.

In mid-October I went to Oslo. A light rain fell, and a blanket of wet fallen leaves clung to the roads. When I complained about the cold, my friend who lives in Oslo told me, "It's not like this in the winter. This isn't cold, it's still warm."

I looked carefully at all the plants as we walked around the city, but there wasn't anything lively enough to catch my eye. I had

forgotten this time of year—what they call "early winter." Plants
may have colorful leaves, but they don't do anything noticeable like
make flowers.

In a park I found clusters of white fruit on the side of a narrow
path. I recognized them. They normally appear here and there in
places like Massachusetts and Europe when it gets this cold. I
looked it up: they are named *Symphoricarpos*, of the honeysuck-
le family, native to North America. It seems "*sympori*" means "to
live with" and "*carpos*" means "fruit." The small white fruit stand
out against the bleak landscape. Because the fruit cling to thin
branches, if you look at them from far away, they look as if they
are floating around in mid-air. They look as if they are grieving the
death of summer. They struggle not to give voice to the loneliness of
being the only ones left. Later, they all decide to sink away quietly,
so quietly.

Here and there around the park trees grow large and spread out,
creating not quite a forest but rather a grove of "Norwegian Wood."
Large branches nearly touch the ground. Branches that will survive
a few more months without a word. It was frustrating that I did
not know any of the trees' names. Maple? Elm? Bodhi tree? In any
case, these were broadleaf trees, and their leaves fell one by one as
I watched. One by one they fell, one by one they piled up.

LOOK, LOOK! IT'S A CACTUS SKELETON!

There are places in the world where it's clearly winter, where it's snowy and icy, where the plants have all died out. I went to Oslo in late autumn, and then I also went to Toronto in in early winter, thinking I would give some thought to the winter season. But each time I returned to Southern California from those places, the sky was blue, the sea was also blue, the palm trees stood out in sharp relief, and the flowers were in full bloom. On top of which, whenever I came back to California, I found it under attack by the Santa Ana winds, which were particularly bad this autumn. So, I quickly forgot about all things winter.

The Santa Anas. They are hot winds that come blowing in from the desert here in Southern California from autumn to winter. The temperature around here is usually a pleasant twenty degrees Celsius, give or take a few degrees. But then suddenly the hot winds start blowing and the temperature goes up close to thirty degrees, and everything dries up. Moisture evaporates from your whole body. Too much evaporates and your body starts floating several centimeters up. The trees and grasses wither, and you start to get forest fires here and there. Even though it's the same thirty-degree temperature as a mellow summer in Kumamoto (you can't say thirty degrees is "hot" in Kumamoto), it feels totally different. It's a thirty degrees Celsius that I can't help but think must be a calculation error that occurred in the conversion from Fahrenheit to Celsius.

At the end of November, I went to Tucson, Arizona. I got on

Interstate Highway 5 from the town where I live and headed south, changed to Highway 8, which runs east to west, and headed due east all the way from there. Highway 8 goes along the border to Mexico. There are check points here and there that stop the flow of traffic, which results in long lines. I was able to make my way slowly and pass through as the inspectors waved me on, but here and there in the inspection areas I saw people with their heads hanging low who were made to get out of their cars and then were surrounded by the inspectors. As soon as I passed through an inspection zone, I sped up and took off.

A wall is visible in the middle of the desert along the part of the highway that runs closest to the border. It's a black wall, cold and indifferent, unlike any wall I've seen around a farm or a factory. It stretched on and on through an area with no sign of life.

The Sonoran Desert extends across a wide area, from the south-eastern part of California to the southwestern part of Arizona, and then on to the area of Mexico called Baja California. The city of Tucson, which sits right in the middle of it, was so hot and dry that it put me on guard—could it be that the Santa Ana winds reach all the way out here? However, when I asked a local old-timer, they told me the weather was unrelated to the Santa Anas and that this was how it always is. It seems that it's usually all dried out here, but for one month in summer they get evening showers. For that month only, dried-up rivers overflow with water and it gets incredibly humid. The old-timer told me that it's really hard to live here when that time comes around.

Among the desert plants, there are those that live communally. They have small, tough leaves and spines. Sharp, painful spines that seem to treat all things in a hostile manner. Even as I write this now, I somehow feel a pricking pain in my foot. I just checked to see—when had I been pricked?—and some spines were hiding in wait within the fabric of my jeans. They had injured my skin, prick, prick, pricking at it. It feels bad. It even feels malicious.

You see a lot of mesquite trees, but they seem dirty somehow. Their bark is rough to the touch and there is no order when it comes to their leaves. The pods that sometimes hang down from them (they belong to the Fabaceae family) seem worn out and crumbly. The trees look as if they are sighing: "There's not enough water and the hard work never ends. There's just no time to worry about appearances."

The palo verde tree, as the name suggests, has a green trunk ("palo verde" means "green stick"); in other words, the whole tree is green, and it's a tree that gives you the impression, at first glance, that it's more of a lizard than a tree. Its leaves are very small, and it often seems that they are not growing even when they are. After a rainfall, they sprout out all at once. In a drought, the leaves fall. If the drought continues on, even the branches fall. I've read that because its leaves are unreliable, the trunk of this green tree is responsible for the whole process of photosynthesis. The trunk looks smooth, like a lizard or moss or those places on crape myrtles where the bark has come off. So I wanted to touch it and see, but when I did, I jumped. The surface was full of thorns. It was as if this tree spoke, crying out: "Don't touch! There's not enough water. We don't have the luxury of being touched by the likes of humans."

When people think of Kumamoto, they think of the bear character mascot named Kumamon. When they think of Arizona, they think of the saguaro cactus. It stands as straight as a pillar, and it grows branches that look like outstretched arms. They're weird, and they stand out. They seem human, like someone in a mascot costume or someone directing traffic.

Shortly after entering Arizona from California, the landscape changed from that of a sandy desert to that of a wasteland. When the saguaro cacti popped into view, I felt moved. Before long, they suddenly increased in number, and in the end, Saguaro cacti covered both sides of the wasteland for as far as the eyes could see. A full field of saguaro cacti. A full field of saguaro cacti. A full field of saguaro cacti. A full field of saguaro cacti. A full field of saguaro cacti. A full field of saguaro cacti. It reminded me of that poem by Yamamura Bochō, where he repeats the line "A full field of rape blossoms" over and over again.

And then there's the barrel cactus. "Barrel cactus" is how they say it in English, in Japanese we call it the "ball cactus." They are short, but they stand out. Barrel is a good name for them; they really do look like barrels, all short and stout and heavy looking. There are ones that spiral and ones that slope downwards. And they are completely covered in spines. Really long spines. Spines that are not so long. Spines that stick straight out. Spines that are curved like fishhooks. They cover the barrel haphazardly.

And then there's the ocotillo. It's a large plant that can grow several meters high. It splits off into many branches from its roots and spreads out in all directions reaching up to the sky.

It's not a cactus, however. It grows in the wasteland, it has spines, and its flowers, which bloom in spring, are really pretty. In other words, it's just like a cactus, but it's not one. Here's the reason why: for a plant to be a cactus, there needs to be something called an areole at the root of its spines, and ocotillo don't have this.

As its long branches sway back and forth in the wasteland, the ocotillo looks as if it were dried out. But it's not. When it rains, it suddenly spouts out green leaves. Just like the palo verde tree. And then in spring, they bloom bright red flowers at the tips of their branches that look like the erect penises of dogs. To put it in different terms, just image a plant that is a composed of the branches of a crown-of-thorns and kombu seaweed from the deep ocean, but all dried out. The flowers, if not compared to a dog's penis, could be said to resemble the flowers of a pomegranate tree. An accidental resemblance, to be sure.

The cholla cactus is hairy, and it's not to be found in bottles of the Choya-brand plum wine that we drink in Japan. It's not thin but it's not fat, and it doesn't stand upright, it just bends all over the place. Because it's hairy and bends all over, it looks like it's moving, but it's not. It's cute, and it looks more like a bunch of stuffed animal arms and legs put together than it does a cactus. But if you look closely, that hair is entirely made up of sinister spines. I was warned by the local old-timer that there is, among the cholla, a type called "jumping cholla," which has spines that arbitrarily jump out at you, and that I should be careful. I thought, "Sure, whatever you say. They're plants. They can't move." But sure enough, I foolishly got too close and got covered in spines. Those spines were so hard to remove and so painful that they made me miserable.

Prickly pear cacti grow all over the place. In the wastelands, and on the sides of roads. They also form hedges in people's yards. And even though they grow everywhere, the ones that get infested with bugs stand out.

A long time ago, I saw a Mexican factory that dyed textiles. The factory was right in the middle of a field of prickly pear cacti. Bugs were densely swarming around the cacti in the field. The field was a nursery for these bugs. They were scale insects called cochineals, and they were quite different from the ones that swarmed around my devil's ivy and monstera plants at home. It seems they have been used since long ago in Aztec and Mayan cultures as a natural ingredient for red pigment, and once the Europeans were taught this, there was a demand for them that equaled that of silver. As someone who has killed innumerable scale insects ever since getting into indoor gardening, this story puts me in a strange frame of mind.

I wondered whether the bugs that swarmed the prickly pears along the side of the road were the same as those precious cochineals, so I caught one and ground it up. I ground it up real good. I ground it so much that you would never think it had been a bug. A dark red liquid dyed my fingers, and then instantly changed color into a fresh-looking rouge on the balls of my fingers.

It's not just cochineals that eat prickly pears—humans do too. The supermarket near our house sells these things that look like prickly pear stems that have had their spines removed. They have a slimly texture and resemble *wakame* seaweed in both flavor and color.

See, there I go again comparing cacti to seaweed. The plants of the wasteland are really very similar to the seaweeds that live at the bottom of the ocean. Standing in the wasteland and looking around, I succumb to the illusion that this is actually the ocean floor, and that these plants are all seaweed.

If you look really, really closely, the wasteland is full of cactus corpses.

Of course, if you go to Sequoia National Forest, you can see trees of every stage of life: young trees, old trees, dead trees, rotting trees. It's the same if you go to a grove of beech trees or a grove of evergreen trees. But the corpses of the cacti in the wasteland, and the changes that befall these corpses minute by minute, are far more graphic than what happens with trees.

Dead saguaro stand and wither in the same posture as living saguaro, their flesh rots and falls away, and they dry out. Before long, many bones begin to stick out from within. Bones that had supported the saguaro for decades, perhaps even for two hundred years. Those bones come sticking out.

Dead cholla lose their spines, lose the flesh from their stems, and eventually become bones full of holes, all while standing in the same posture as living cholla.

In Buddhism, there is a practice of contemplating the process by which a human corpse decomposes. It's called *Hakkotsukan* or "white-bone viewing." These cacti living tough here in the Sonoran

Desert, could it be that they are practicing this meditation? I won't go so far as to claim that this is the case, but I will say they embody the practice.

If you think about it, the wild excitement of the Mexican "Day of the Dead," a day in which you can cross paths with skeletons, resembles the cactus way of life. And the writing of Juan Rulfo, in which living humans mingle with dead humans as they walk across the wasteland—his literary works that seem to represent the land of Mexico—are they not, themselves, also cacti?

THE MIRACULOUS WELWITSCHIAS
OF BERLIN

What I witnessed in Arizona was the cactus way of life—a way of life that sits side by side with death. There, death was cheerful and indifferent. The smell of death even attracted animals that would eat the rotting flesh.

I had begun thinking seriously about "winter" while visiting Oslo and Toronto, and I continued thinking about it until I went to Arizona, where my thinking was completely interrupted. While still in this state of interruption, I went to Berlin. It was the middle of December. Berlin's in the north, and it's inland, so I thought surely it must be cold, and prepared accordingly. Sure enough, it was really cold. It dropped below freezing, and snow fell, turning everything bright white. The wind blew right through the down jacket I had bought in Southern California, and the gloves I had bought at a 100-yen store in Japan were completely useless in the face of the freezing snow. Having no choice, I wore what I had and walked around outdoors all bundled up.

I had looked forward to this: visiting Berlin and seeing all the plants in the middle of a true winter. Everything dying out ruthlessly, with no signs of life anywhere to be found. In the fields of Toronto at the beginning of November, I had seen trees and grasses that were destined for such ruthlessness, like the sumacs (which belong to the Anacardiaceae family) that had gone to seed and stood there all dried out, and the white birches that had turned completely white, as if to say: "Look, look! This is my bark!" There was a sense of approaching death that hung around these plants that pointed, without fail, to them be swallowed up by winter, freezing through and dying off, corpses strewn all over the place . . . I had hoped for this.

I lived in Poland a long time ago. It must have been cold, but I don't remember. I was young, so maybe it wasn't cold to me. I would walk steadily along a dark snow-covered street to a bus stop, ride the bus to my place of business, then walk steadily along a dark snow-covered street, and get back on the bus and head home. Dawn just didn't seem to break, and the sun would set early. No sunlight whatsoever would shine through the winter season. Every building had a door inside of the door that served as the entrance from the outside, where a bulky curtain would hang that would block the outside air from coming in. Before going inside, you would take off everything you had in front of the curtain and hand it over to the sullen-faced person working the coat check, and when you would leave, you'd hand them some small change and they'd retrieve your mountain of clothing, and then you'd start over from square one, putting everything back on, and then head out. I do remember all of these things.

But what I remember even better than all of that is getting through the winter (which surely must have been cold) and spring finally arriving, and how even though there was still snow on the ground, crocuses would pop right up in a corner of the park, and then how you'd get deeper into spring and freshly harvested green beans would suddenly appear in shop windows, and the joy of eating them boiled and covered in yogurt (which is to say that in winter all you could get your hands on were things like root vegetables and shriveled-up apples and pickled cabbage), and the bright shine of the berries that would begin to appear all lined up in the street stalls, and the sweetness of picking those berries up

in your fingers and popping them in your mouth—I remember all
of this very clearly.

And so, Berlin. It was the darkest period of the year, in the mid-
dle of December. But I didn't see corpses strewn all over the place.
To be sure, it was cold, it was below freezing, and it snowed. Days
grew shorter by the hour, and no sunlight shone through. Trees and
grasses were covered in a snow that crushed them.

A friend of mine that lives in Berlin took me to the botanical gar-
dens attached to the Free University in the Dahlem neighborhood.
This friend and I go way back, so she knows all about my passion
for plants. The gardens were somewhere I really wanted to visit
ever since hearing about them while I was in Japan two years prior.

My friend's father had been a missionary, and he had lived a
long time in the southern African country of Namibia. My friend
visited him many times and saw something truly miraculous in
the Namibia desert. I say "desert," but it's a wasteland-like place
where scattered grasses grow, and a place where far in the distance
something grows thick and dense. Way over there. Over there, too.
Seen from far away, they look like trash heaps. But when you get
closer, you see that they're plants. Withered leaves with pointy tips
that are wrapped up in coils. My friend said there are some of these
plants that have been alive since the time of Jesus Christ, and that
they have some in a botanical garden in Berlin, and that I should
come see them.

In early spring two years back, my friend visited Kumamoto. It
was right after the big earthquake. I showed her around, and when
we went to Aso, we saw that the water sources famous to the area
had been transformed. There are places where water bubbles up
from the side of the mountain. The wet rock face was covered in
ferns and lichens, and water would suddenly come spurting out,
creating a new flow. A year ago, however, the rock face was com-
pletely dry. The amount of water was about equal to a faucet left

running. I took water from that gentle trickle into my hands and drank some; the flavor should have been soft, but it had become hardened. I had heard that a lake in the town of Aso had dried up overnight, and when I went to take a look, all of the plants that had been underwater were now left exposed. Once they dried out on land, these plants that had been all slippery and swayed fiercely under the water became mere dried grass.

From there we climbed up to the mouth of the volcano that is Mount Aso. The natural pools of hot water that had always been there had disappeared. A person monitoring the area told us it had been that way for about a month now. Just then a loud announcement echoed forth, and while I understood something was wrong, I couldn't catch what the announcement was saying. I asked the person working there, who was getting ready to leave, what the announcement was about, and they told me that the concentration of sulfur dioxide in the steam that was blowing up from the volcano had reached a dangerous level. We hurried back to the car and drove away from the mouth of Mount Aso.

It was during this trip that my friend told me about the miraculous plant, and about the botanical garden in Berlin.

It's named welwitschia. It's a gymnospermous plant of the Welwitschiaceae family, within the Gnetopsida division of plants. The name "welwitschia" comes from the name of the European who discovered it. The Japanese name for it is "*sabaku-omoto*," which means "desert rohdea." Or it's called "*kisōtengai*," which is also an adjective that means "fantastic," "miraculous," or "bizarre." The fact that the name for this plant uses such "fantastic" Chinese characters (rather than phonetic katakana) is a trait shared with succulents, as I have already discussed.

I arranged a visit to Berlin in March of last year. I fully planned on seeing the welwitschia. I had to cancel the trip at the last moment, however, for a number of reasons. It was truly a shame. However,

I was able, quite unexpectedly, to finally visit Berlin this winter.

The botanical garden was enormous. There was a shiny glass greenhouse that towered over everything. It was giant, with a round ceiling and exposed steel beams that covered its glass surface. And it had extensions built off it, one after another, like an old hot springs resort in Japan. The plants were assembled thematically, and they were growing luxuriously. You would open a door, and then the flora of a whole new region would spread out in front of you, seeming as if it might continue on forever.

I was led along by my friend, and we ran through South America, which was wrapped in vines; we ran through the cacti-filled desert of North America; we ran through the Asian bamboo grove; we ran through the Japanese camellia grove, and the begonias, and the orchids, too. We even ran through the carnivorous plants.

And then, there they were, in a small, special room. In the center of this glass exhibition room that looked like it was made of bay windows. The plants in this room looked like they were being kept alive as scientific specimens. No, actually, all of the plants in the gardens looked like this, but I just hadn't noticed as they went on thriving and wilting away. I only noticed the specimen-like quality of the plants in this room alone, this room with plants entirely from the Namibian desert. Among them the welwitschia. There were only seven of them, both small and large ones. The big ones had stems about the size of a human baby's head. You could call it a "stem," but it was more of a lump that resembled a rock with a gaping crack down the middle. The small ones were like those model teeth you see at the dentist. From these grew several leaves that resembled kombu seaweed. The leaves had grown and then withered at the tip, but the base of each leaf, which were close to the stem, were fresh and green, and they looked like they were wriggling around. I felt like I had seen something like this before, and then I realized—it resembled Futakuchi-onna, that mythical *yōkai* spirit with two mouths. Futakuchi-onna has one mouth on her face and one on the back of her head—a head that splits apart as the second mouth is revealed. It's said that she uses her hair-like tentacles to feed herself rice in both mouths. And now, I was looking at a plant that looked like it was doing the same thing. Its leaves were more long and thin than they were flat. It looked like there were several of them, but actually there were only two. They were broken up and ripped apart, and so they looked like more than two leaves. This is a unique characteristic of this plant—it only grows two leaves its whole life, and it grows them endlessly. Even more so than the cacti of Arizona, the welwitschia looks like seaweed. Right in the middle of the Namibian desert.

For what reason did it come to resemble seaweed? Does it come to long for an ocean it has never seen, the more dried out it gets? I would ask the plant itself if it could give me an answer.

After seeing the welwitschia, we headed outside. "It's a blizzard," I said, but my friend responded, "This is no blizzard. It's just snowing." "But it's so cold, and the snow just keeps falling and falling," I said, but my friend responded, "This is still nowhere near a blizzard." So I summoned up some courage and walked on, through a section of the garden that was landscaped with Japanese plants. There were several cherry trees, but they were totally bare. My friend told me that one year in spring, she tried doing the Japanese custom of *hanami* or "flower viewing" under the flowers of these trees. She brought rice balls and saké in a thermos, but she was immediately scolded and chased off by someone who worked in the garden. I asked: "What's that tree? And that one over there?" My friend answered my questions about each tree, but not a single one of them had any leaves left. But there was a *Callicarpa japonica* that was covered in berries (named *Murasaki shikibu* in Japanese, after the writer of *The Tale of Genji*). The berries were that deep, refined purple that is characteristic of the plant.

The white berries of the *Symphoricarpos*, or snowberry, had been growing in Oslo when I visited. Red berries grow in the fields of California, they grow in bunches. And now again, within the snow of Berlin—the *Callicarpa japonica*. Oh, the lustrous beauty of those berries. That color that makes you want to bring your hands together in praise of fall and winter—all berries. They take the summer sunlight, and life itself, and condense them into color.

And then we arrived in a section of the garden full of plants from the west coast of North America. In this section, there was a young giant sequoia.

My friend said, "To someone from North America, it must look like a kindergartener." Well, even if it did look young enough to wear a diaper, I of course fixed my gaze on it. Although young, it grew straight up with that red bark that I was used to seeing.

The snow was coming down. It piled up on my hat and eyelids. Snow piled up on the shoulders of someone we passed who was walking their dog. It piled up on the back of the dog, too. German people are amazing—in the middle of such stormy weather, they walked about, bundling their babies up in clothing and pushing them around in carriages. And the babies slept soundly. Snow piled up on top of the carriages, and also on top of the babies' cheeks. There is a poem by Miyoshi Tatsuji that reads:

> Snow falls and piles on Tarō's roof, sending Tarō to sleep.
> Snow falls and piles on Jirō's roof, sending Jirō to sleep. [2]

Snow fell and piled up in this place that did not belong to either Tarō or Jirō. But it's strange. Nothing about it felt threatening.

Just the other day, I read Shibata Motoyuki's translation of Jack London's *To Build a Fire*. Actually, I bought the book after a moving experience of hearing the translator read aloud from the Japa-

THE MIRACULOUS WELWITSCHIAS OF BERLIN 93

nese, so the story first came to me through my ears. It's a story of a man who loses his way in the middle of the snow. He seemed cold. It seemed as if death was pulling him in. Nothing existed there, not even any plants. A dog was the only living thing around.

However, in this real-life winter of Berlin, because I've been thinking of nothing but plants as of late, even in the middle of this incessant snowfall, I feel as if . . . Ahh . . . I feel as if my body fluids have become tree sap, and that, at times, I am undergoing photosynthesis through my hair. And so, even as the snow fell upon me endlessly, I felt fully alive, with no sense of death. The more the snow piled up on my head, and the colder and number my fingers became, the more confidence I had that something bright and warm was on its way, and that I would be revived.

I had thought that the islands of Amakusa off the west coast of Kumamoto would be warm and full of light, but this was not the case at all. It was terribly cold. There was even a light snowfall. The wind was incredibly strong, and standing on top of the bluffs, I was scared that it would carry me out to the open sea. The temperature was probably around five to six degrees Celsius (or low forties in Fahrenheit), but because of the strong wind and my light clothing (which is typical dress for Kumamoto), it felt as if it were below freezing. I should have faced the weather in the same kind of heavy winter clothing that I had worn in Berlin and Oslo.

Once, long ago, I took a boat from the San Diego Bay out a little way into the open sea to go whale watching. The wind was incredibly strong, and it was terribly cold. On land, it was the usual warm California, so passengers were wearing tank-tops and shorts. I, too, was wearing similarly light clothing, and so I was exposed to the harsh wind. It was more painful than it was cold, and I was shocked to think that being a sailor, or a pirate, or a drifter could be this intense.

I felt exactly the same way at the coast of Amakusa. I had underestimated it. I was careless.

I cut across a mountain road from the city of Hondo on Amakusa Shimoshima, and right as I came out on the west side of the island, the waves of the East China Sea swelled. The surface of the water looked as if the tips of the waves were scattered about and inlayed with white stars, each shining brightly.

It was afternoon. The sun was high in the western sky. West, beyond the sea. Light streamed through the clouds and onto the surface of the sea in a radial pattern. It looked like a spotlight, but it was directed at nothing—there was just the rustling sea that couldn't calm down for even a moment, and the shining crests of waves.

The Nishibira Camellia Park on the island of Amakusa Shimoshima. I wanted to see the camellias in full bloom in winter. The camellia festival was supposed to be happening soon, so I figured there would be a big crowd. I went to go check it out, all the while complaining to myself foolishly about how many people were sure to be there. Instead, I found this cold weather. There were no flowers in bloom. There were people making camellia oil in the offices of the camellia park, but that was the only sign of human life. The camellia festival was a long, long ways off.

I'd been mistaken. It's the *Camellia sasanqua* (*sazanka* in Japanese) that blooms in winter, not regular camellia (*tsubaki*). The mountains of Amakusa, which were meant to be perpetually green, looked brown in winter, even without the trees losing their leaves, as if they had sunken into a deep silence.

Amakusa is comprised of multiple islands. To the north is the Ariake Sea, home to Mount Unzen, and to the west is the rough East China Sea. To the east, unidentified volcanoes penetrate into the inlets and bays, and spread out quietly. If you take National Highway 57 west from Kumamoto City, it suddenly stops being called Highway 57 around Mitsumi Harbor on the coast. They say you can cross the ocean and go all the way to Nagasaki, arriving in Shimabara, but I've never confirmed this. After Mitsumi Harbor, the highway turns into a prefectural road. With the same width, and the same amount of traffic, it winds along the coast with one lane per side.

You cross five bridges. From Ōyanoshima to Kamishima, then Shimoshima. The road that runs along the coast of the Ariake Sea

carefully stiches together the outer edges of each island. On this
occasion, I passed through Hondomachi and went inland. *Camel-
lia sasanqua* bloomed in clusters on the road that cut through the
inland mountains. They were in full bloom. From this inland road
full of tunnels, all of a sudden, I ended up on a road that followed
the coastline. The mountains butted right up along the East China
Sea, as if they were about to fall into it. The sea had changed from
the Ariake Sea, with its mirror-like stillness, to the open ocean of
the East China Sea.

The difference between *Camellia sasanqua* (*sazanka*) and *tsubaki*
is a difference of blooming season (a difference I now understood
as it penetrated into my flesh and bones), and also a difference of
appearance.

Sazanka flowers open wide, and their pistils and stamens come
popping out. No, actually, that's not really the case. It only seems
that way because I'm comparing them to the pure-bred camellias.
There exist a large number of crossbreeds between *sazanka* and
tsubaki. There are *sazanka* that closely resemble *tsubaki*, and there
are *tsubaki* that closely resemble *sazanka*. There are also *tsubaki*
that open their mouths wide and expose their pistols and stamen.

But the biggest difference between the two is in how they end
up. Those that drop each petal one by one with a plop are *tsubaki*.
Those that scatter them around into the wind are *sazanka*.

The flower trees that appeared on the coastal road that cut inland
all had petals scattered underneath them. I've heard that there are,
among the crossbreeds, *sazanka* flowers that drop their petals like
tsubaki, but I won't get into the minute details. What in the world is
the difference between *sazanka* and *tsubaki*, these flowers that look
so much alike and crossbreed so often? If it's a difference like the
one between coyotes and dogs, then they can reproduce no matter
how much they crossbreed. They are both of the Theaceae family,
of the genus *Camellia*, and so they are related to the tea plant. They

all look a lot alike, down to the color and shape of their flowers. Really, really similar.

In the camellia park, there is a grove of wild camellias; they say about 20,000 of them grow there naturally. One of the men making camellia oil, S-san, agreed to be my guide. According to S-san, the park used to be a pine forest once upon a time. The trees had been used to build the shaft for a coal mine. But they became infested with insects, and little by little they died off. They completely died off about forty years before I visited. And then the camellia, which had been growing in the underbrush, stretched their way up.

The grove was completely covered in camellias. There were large boulders and stones towering throughout, and camellia trees came growing out endlessly from the small spaces between them. There were some here and there that had flowers attached to them. There were some that had seeds hanging off them. On the ground, there had fallen many hard, round fruits. There were some that had split open as they fell. If you looked closely, you'd see many hard, black seeds had also fallen here and there. S-san explained, using the local dialect:

"If you head down to the lower part, there're some big old trees. They got bent by the wind, and they're all curved sideways-like."

Because S-san had invited me to do so, I followed him down.

There was an observation deck along the way. Standing there, all I saw was the East China Sea, everywhere I looked. Camellia trees stretched out all the way to the sea. They'd all been flattened, beaten down by the wind.

There were some large trees here and there. I asked if a certain tree was old, but I was told that I was mistaken. I was told it was a *muku* tree (and that you could tell because it had a different kind of trunk). We climbed further down, with S-san pointing out trees along the way: "This one's a camphor, and that one's a sea fig. That one's camphor, too, and that one's a *gajomaru* (and it's called *ga-*

jomaru, not *gajumaru*). That's a zelkova (which you can tell because it's lost all its leaves)."

S-san stopped in front of the zelkova and climbed up and over the stone trellis along the path to get closer to the tree. He rubbed the tree's trunk, and with deep admiration he explained: "The branches come sprouting out and split up and keep growing. Then they return to the original branch, and they become one again." Like the branches of a ficus or a pachira, the zelkova's branches had come together. You could make out the faint seams where they attached to one another. From there they grew out even more and then came back together. You could see those seams as well. Full of such seams, the trunk twisted and turned as it grew.

"Come look, see here," S-san was insistent, so I too crossed over the path and approached the tree. I touched it. It felt amazing. It was smooth like skin. I wouldn't say it possessed its own body temperature, but it was much warmer than the air temperature that surrounded it. Its trunk was white. A variety of colors came floating out of the depths of that whiteness. Green, red, yellow—it would be like seeing through to its veins and internal organs, if it were human. The whiteness of the bark and the coloration of these organs overlapped and appeared elegant and seductive. I felt as if it were cuddling up to me.

It was as if I were caressing someone's arm, but because the arm is not really a sexual part of the body, I'd never had someone to caress in this way before, not until this moment. But now I had found one. It was that kind of feeling. It also felt like the tree had told me to caress it and so I was doing as I was told.

All the leaves were gathered together up near the top of the tree, and so the arm felt hairless. But it didn't seem ashamed, like men who lose their hair as they age. The several-meter-tall tree was not large nor wide, but rather thin as it branched off and grew out. Like the other camellia trees, it had been deformed by the wind. Like the other camellia trees, it was covered in brown kudzu vines.

Up to this point, my eyes turned only toward large trees. I hadn't imagined that small trees, too, were able to conserve so much energy as the years went by. S-san told me that as camellias reach around one hundred years in age, they stop producing seeds. He said these camellia trees were close to two hundred years old. If so, they probably will not produce any more seeds. I would like to confirm this at some point when the flowering season arrives, either this year or next, it doesn't really matter when. Will they bloom flowers? Will they scatter their blossoms?

Camellia trees covered the entire slope that reached down to the sea. Camellias covered over everything, the tops of which were covered themselves by dried-up creeping kudzu vines.

"Those vines, you cut 'em at the roots and they come right back. They're persistent, too much to handle, but I guess that's nature for you."

S-san continued explaining that even though they were all dried up at the moment, come spring they'd sprout new buds and cover up and hide everything in their path. But even still, the camellia are strong and so they won't dry out. Well, sometimes there are a few that do, but overall, they don't.

"It's cold today, huh? The wind's blowing from the northwest. Before long the *haenkaze* will come blowing from the right side of Ōgase."

S-san said this to the friend I had brought along with me. This friend was born and raised in Amakusa and had taken me around the area many, many times before, showing me the rock formations in the East China Sea, the best spots for sunsets over the waves, the tree groves, all kinds of hidden spots. S-san was an old acquaintance of theirs.

"'*Haenkaze*' is what we call the southeastern wind," my friend explained, turning to me. With that, I recalled the *Butsurui shōko*, a dialect dictionary complied by haiku poet Koshigaya Gozan in the eighteenth century. Words related to wind were collected at the beginning of the book. There were many words among them that call wind "*hae*," like "*shirahae*" and "*kurohae*." They all meant "southern wind." This was my first time hearing the word used in everyday conversation.

Ōgase, a rock formation made of many pillar-shaped reefs, was floating out at sea right before our eyes.

S-san said that there was a coral reef out there, that all kinds of fish gathered around it, that soon the evening sun would sink down between those stones, that it was amazing, that it was beautiful. But we stood on an observation deck, windswept, where my hair was being noisily whipped around to the left and right and up and down, covering my face and covering my ears, so I couldn't make out S-san's Amakusa dialect. But I could make out clearly what it was he meant.

The sea at Amakusa was rough. The peaks of the waves shone brilliantly. Light bloomed forth. A black kite cried out from the sky. It cried out again. Through a crack in the sky, the evening sun pierced through, dazzlingly.

BAOBAB DREAM

People I know in Japan said that it was cold there. They said it again and again before I went, and they continue to say it now that I've returned home.

And so I went to Kumamoto with the only clothing I own that is meant to withstand the cold: the down jacket I had worn in Berlin and Toronto. But Kumamoto was not cold. There was some coldness, but it was the gentle kind. Only once did I wish I had been wearing that down jacket, when I stood exposed to the wind at the edge of the platform at the Amakusa Camellia Park. Other than that, the word "down" never even crossed my mind.

The forecast called for heavy snow in Tokyo. People in Tokyo said that flights in and out of the city might be disrupted. But there was no heavy snow, no accumulation whatsoever, and my plane flew right on schedule. I left my down jacket at a friend's house in Tokyo without wearing it even once and returned home to Southern California.

It was warm when I got there. The sunlight was bright. I started feeling that somehow, somewhere along the way I had been tricked. Each of the plants in my home wore an exhausted expression. I was exhausted, too, and I gazed off absentmindedly into the distance. I casually picked up a pot with devil's ivy in it. It was all dried out, too dry, like the shed skin of some snake. Panicked, I soaked it with water and looked around the house. Everywhere I looked there were plants that required emergency treatment.

I watered. I soaked the plants that were overly dry. Bugs were crawling all over the homalomena. I plucked off its leaves, covered with scale insects, and resolutely broke off its flowers and small buds. The entire root stock, with its many crevices, I washed by hand with electrolyzed water, massaging it with my fingertips. Leaf by leaf, stem by stem, the underside of each leaf, each crack on each stem—I washed clean every nook and cranny. I threw away a few pots and put a few others in shady spots in the house where the sunlight never reaches.

I have, by nature, a passion for tending to indoor plants. One day about ten years back, when I had already been through the cycle of buying them and having them dry out and wither away, I picked up a massive encyclopedia of gardening that was in our house (it seems that my husband had bought it once upon a time). It was called *House Plant*, just like the name of that story I wrote. It was so heavy that I had to hold it with both of my arms. I started reading it. Once I started consulting the book and using it to help take care of the plants, they stopped wilting. It was fascinating. Before long, I was able to know, more or less, how to take care of a certain plant by looking up its scientific family name and place of origin. I was able to keep it alive for months and years, even when its conditions worsened, without having it wilt and die. At one point, we had around two hundred potted plants lined up inside the house, and every day I did nothing but remove dried leaves off them and transplant them from one pot to another.

In those days, there wasn't a plant nursery around with any plant that I would be unable to recognize. It was fun picking out which potted plants were in good condition, but it was also fun buying the ones in not-so-great condition and then bringing them back to good health. Soaking the tips of their branches in water, they would start to multiply. Glass bottles full of water would line our windowsills. When they were used up, I would start using cups. My family started complaining.

I took care of a lot of plants, but a lot of them withered and died. There were also many that I refused to let live, whose roots and tendrils I snipped away at with my own hands. To a certain degree, this is inevitable when you put out plants as decorations in your home—you have to give up, and you have no choice but to throw them away, to let them wither, to kill them. This I knew from daily practice.

It was around that time that I discovered the cosmic law of plant life. That the way of living and dying is different for plants and animals (including humans). That plants don't die even when they die, that dying is living, that living is not dying.

It was a rainy winter in California. There was a major wildfire the year before and everything burned: the mountains, the fields, the forests. In the spring following the rainy winter, everything that had been burnt and lost in the fire, all of it, came back to life.

It was also around that time that I went to Sequoia National Park for the first time. My youngest daughter was around seven years old. I was certain I wouldn't give birth to another child. I took the last of my children by the hand and we stood in front of a giant sequoia. As we looked up, pinecones came raining down. I saw many young sequoias sprouting up around the vicinity. I was in my forties, and would not give birth again, perhaps *could not* give birth again. And yet these two-thousand-some-odd-year-old giant trees were still able to give birth, and were right in the middle of giving birth. Right then and there, I felt as if the cosmic law of plants that I had understood up to that point had ascended to the next stage of evolution.

A little while after that, my father developed stomach cancer. My mother had a stroke. I spent less time in Japan when I went back. Every time I did go back, I was greeted by plants that I had left behind, which had withered in my absence.

For a few years, I went back and forth between Japan and California almost every month. I would be away from home for several weeks at a time. The plants were neglected. The weak ones gradually withered away. The sturdy ones, the ones without bugs, the ones that were drought tolerant—only these survived. Plants in the Araceae family, like monstera, anthurium, and devil's ivy, are generally strong. Snake plant is too, as are plants in the Asparagaceae family. Spurges, too, and the whole Euphorbiaceae family. The Lamiaceae family is strong, too, and so is the Commelinaceae family.

During a recent absence, scale insects appeared on many plants (though not on the homalomena). The plectranthus that I had kept alive for so long finally met its end. The tradescantia, which always came back to life no matter how many times it died, also met its end, and I threw it away. I trimmed off its leaves and then threw it away. The tropical pitcher plant called *Nepenthes rafflesiana* was also beyond repair.

Herein lies another cosmic law of potted plants: they are at their most beautiful when you first purchase them, and they get progressively shabbier and shabbier, even if you take care of them. And then, at some point, they wither away and die.

The house became empty. And so, for the first time in a long while, I went shopping at the garden store. A small fittonia. A medium-sized phlebodium. A medium-sized syngonium. A small philodendron and a hanging pot to put it in. Several aeoniums, thinking I'd put them in the sunny spot on a windowsill, and geranium, oxalis, and ranunculus, thinking it would be nice to have some with flowers. I felt like a hunter, out for blood. I was going overboard and filling my cart when something caught my eye: a large tree sitting in a large ceramic pot that was around thirty dollars.

I didn't know what kind of tree it was, but it was so cheap given its size and the fact that it was in a ceramic pot, that I felt disoriented. Without thinking it over, I put it in my cart and paid for it. When it came time to put it in my car, I realized the car I drove to the store was too small and it wouldn't fit inside. So I called my youngest daughter, Tomé, and asked her to bring the bigger car, and she helped me bring it home. Along the way, she admonished me: "Aren't you the one always saying that we shouldn't make impulse purchases?"

I looked it up once I got home. It was a big plant, one I wasn't familiar with. I thought it resembled a pachira, but that wasn't quite right, so I carefully looked up plants in the same family, Bombacaceae (the Malvaceae family within the APG [Angiosperm Phylogeny Group] system). And then I got the strong feeling that it might be a baobab.

I found an image of a young baobab plant, which looked like a small, furry sprout. The picture and the large, unfamiliar tree I had brought home were like two peas in a pod. I searched for more photos and found one of a full-grown baobab standing tall in the middle of an African savannah. There was also a sketch from *The Little Prince*, of baobab trees consuming the stars. The baobab wasn't just a tall tree, it was a wide one, with volume, so much volume. It had a terrifying face and looked extremely heavy.

I looked at the images and was horrified. . . . I thought to myself, "What am I gonna do with this thing? This isn't a savannah." As I sat there shuddering, I felt a gust of wind blow through the house and pass through my heart. But the baobab sitting in the pot was a young plant, and the sad thing was that it would probably wither and die before it ever got that big. The fate of the house plant. When it comes down to it, house plants are at their most beautiful when you first purchase them, and they get progressively shabbier and shabbier. They get weak and then soon enough they wither and die. I decided to protect it the best I could for as long as I could, and for the time being moved it to the sunniest spot I could find.

But when I took a really, really close look at it, I realized I was wrong. It resembled a *Schefflera* more than any "baobab." It resembled a *yatsude* (or *Fatsia japonica*). It resembled an Australia umbrella tree. If that's the case, then it's of the Araliaceae family. Generally speaking, both *yatsude* and Australia umbrella trees grow large in in their native soil. But somehow, they just weren't as interesting. They didn't really move me, emotionally speaking. No wind could pass through.

Lording over the savannahs of Africa, swallowing up the stars— such things would be possible were the tree a "baobab," but I had the feeling these were things neither the *yatsude* nor the Australia umbrella tree could accomplish.

Here's a story from long ago. A pet shop in Kumamoto had a wallaby for sale, and I wanted to buy it so badly. It was about the size of an Akita, and it cost around $5,000. I had about that much to spend, as I had been planning on buying a (small) car. I thought, wouldn't it be so refreshing to have a wallaby hopping around inside my house—a house full of stuffiness borne of midlife crisis? Wouldn't it transform my home into the breezy grasslands of Australia? I had a brief moment of indecision, thinking maybe I should not buy a car and instead buy the wallaby, but I was warned by my daughter (by which I mean Kanoko, my oldest, who was around ten years old at the time), who said to me with a stern look on her face: "You'll definitely regret it, so you shouldn't buy it." I came to my senses.

The dream remains a dream. I can't figure out the true identity of the tree. But my daughters and I, we all call it "the baobab." "The baobab" drinks a lot of water.

Plants are really hard to identify. It's not easy to know the name of some grass you discover along the roadside just from its shape. It's different with animals. A dog is a dog, a cat a cat, you know right away . . .

Plus, plants these days, their scientific names have changed. Like this "baobab" for instance, it was in the Bombacaceae family according to the old system of categorization, but in the new APG system it's in the Malvaceae family. I'm not terribly familiar with the Bombacaceae family, so it's not such a big deal, but the new version of the very familiar Liliaceae family—that's a real problem.

The original Liliaceae family was such a large hodgepodge that you'd think: "Huh? Are all of these really in the same family?" To give some familiar examples: tiger lily, lily of the valley, tulip, aloe, dwarf mondo grass, green onion, St. Bernard's lily—all of these belonged to the Liliaceae family. However, within the APG system, the Liliaceae family was shattered into tiny pieces, and separated out into a number of families with names that sound incomprehensible to me, like the Agavaceae family, and the Asparagaceae family, and the Amaryllidaceae family. It's like spiders scattering when you turn on the light, or some kind of pointless pissing contest. It's excessive, and even though it's not my problem, I feel bewildered by it.

I've always loved plants, even since I was a child, way back when. While I walked around with a botanical field guide in hand, my gaze pointed downward, chasing after the grasses with my eyes, trying to find out what this one was and what that one was, I grew into an adult. Plant names and scientific names, they're childhood friends. So while the shattering of the Liliaceae family leaves me feeling bewildered like the time a friend's family was torn apart due to bankruptcy and said friend then collapsed due to illness, all I can do is keep a close watch.

I was indoors, thinking of such things, when I suddenly noticed that the outdoors was in the full bloom of California springtime. In the park next door, the mountain lilacs were at their peak. The peach trees and plum trees and cherry trees were blooming in folks' yards. The roadsides were bright yellow from the acacias. The bushes of sweet-scented geranium in my own garden, too, had suddenly grown dense and were so thick that they seemed to be sweating, steeped in a green that surrounded one or two pink buds—swelling with each coming day and trying to open up any minute now.

EUCRYPTA CAME WALKING

Two years ago, I discovered a thicket of really cute leaves behind our neighborhood park, Cottonwood Creek, and planned on transplanting them. The park is next to the sea, and a small stream runs through it, with many shrubs that resemble cottonwoods lining the stream. In early spring, silk-like silver flowers blow in the wind. I wondered, since it's right next to the ocean, whether those flowers, and the river stream itself, might also be salty.

The interior of the park is kept up beautifully, with a wide lawn, playground equipment that reflects the sunlight, a play area made of soft ground so that children won't hurt themselves if they fall off of the playground equipment, flowerbeds full of blooming plants, water fountains, picnic benches, all kinds of things that show how considerate they were with the design—so it's the best park to bring children to. But if you make your way to the back of the park where the stream flows, there's a dirt path that nobody uses, lined on both sides by cottonwoods. (I don't know the real name of these trees. I think they belong to the same family as willows.) There are cattails growing there, too, and all kinds of other plants growing: Asteraceaes, Poaccaes, Liliaceaes, Onagraceaes, Scrophulariaceaes. The whole area is covered with the vines of wild gourds. And then there is a grove of eucalyptus trees that were planted there long, long ago and then grew large and wild, dropping flower pedals and hard seeds. That's the kind of place it is.

The leaves I found were growing in the shade of these large eucalyptus trees, sprouting up in a moderately damp location where the morning sun could still reach. At first glance, they were fine and delicate like ferns, or even somewhat like chamomile flowers or young mugwort leaves. They were bright green and utterly fresh. They had that sweetness about them that is characteristic of young things, but it also seemed like they would hold on to that sweetness even as they matured.

I wanted to bring some of these plants home with me and hoped that they would spread throughout my garden. I dug with my fingertips, and their thin roots came up easily. I protected them in one of the plastic bags that I always brought along to pick up dog poop (I was mid-walk at the time) and gently planted them in the shade of the pepper tree in the front yard. But it was of no use. They up and disappeared on me.

These things happen. I went back to the spot where I had found the leaves many times. Sometimes they were there, sometimes they weren't. I figured this must change with the seasons, but I wasn't sure. In any case, taking the dogs for a walk was my primary objective, so even if I saw some plants while walking, I would forget about them by the time I returned home. And so, time passed.

I suddenly realized just how much time had passed. What made me realize this was the fact that other things started to catch my attention around the area that I had noticed those leaves—things like the white jasmine that shot up suddenly in spring and started blooming even though it was surrounded by dried-up coils of brown vines and leaves; and the various lilies that started sprouting leaves (the ones the gophers live off of); and the sweet-scented geranium, so full of green buds, that started lifting its heavy head. It was spring, and these things all caught my eye.

One day I noticed, in the half-shade of my front lawn, what looked like those leaves that had disappeared on me. Were they really spreading out in that spot? I couldn't believe it. As I stared in disbelief, I saw they had even bloomed some flowers. Sweet, small little white flowers. They were blooming here and there on top of the thicket of leaves. They were so small that I wouldn't have noticed them if I wasn't wearing my glasses. Each flower had five petals that formed a cup-like shape.

It was miraculous to think that they had taken root a year after I first planted them. I figured the roots that remained underground must have been growing slowly, even after they dried out above ground, and sprouted up through the soil when the right season arrived. But more than that, I got the impression that they had slowly, oh so slowly, walked on over from the park.

The plants came walking.

It was my youngest daughter, Tomé, who said this. She wasn't young enough to believe such fairy tales, but she started saying this one day out of the blue. I was laughing, thinking it was a funny thing to say, but then both of our expressions turned serious. I had the feeling that something like what Tomé said had actually happened. And so Tomé explained, with great care, the experience of the plants:

"Once upon a time, a woman was passing through the back end of the park. She looked our way and complimented us: 'How cute! So cute.' She dug up one or two of our comrades and took them away. The comrades she took with her dried up and disappeared. These things happen in the plant world. It's not like the kind of death that you find in the animal world. It's just that our existence slides, from over here to over there, from over there to another spot. That's all. But, that woman did well by us. And so, we had to repay her kindness, even if we were just plants.

"Several of us made an arrangement, and in the middle of the night we quietly snuck out of the park and started walking to the woman's house. The road was a big one, full of cars passing by. In the afternoon, a strong sunlight beat down, drying everything up. There were those of us that collapsed and dried up along the way. There were those of us that kept on walking, even after wilting. We kept on walking with all of our might. Because plants do not usually walk, we had to stop and pretend to be growing anytime a person walked by. Once they passed by, we would begin walking once again. This is how it went for us, and so even though the house was only a five-minute drive by car, it took us, with our tiny plant legs, a whole year . . ."

And then it was my turn. Since they had found their way to my home, I wanted to take good care of the plants. To do so, I would need to learn their name. First and foremost, I would need to pinpoint their scientific name. Then I would be able to understand their true character, like whether they like full sun or shade, or how much water they prefer.

But I had no idea. They weren't a type of fern. Nor were they a type of aster. Looking at their flowers, I could see that they were cute and tidy, but there are plenty of flowers out there that are cute and tidy. Even a novice can identify a flower if it's in the legume family, or the fern family, or the arum family. But sadly, this plant was none of these. Nor was it a figwort or some kind of primrose. This being the case, I took to searching for it on the internet as if I were engaged in carpet bombing, looking up flowers one after another. And then suddenly I happened upon it. The flower looked similar. So did the shape. It belonged to the Boraginaceae family.

And so I found it. *Eucrypta chrysanthemifolia* of the Boraginaceae family. Sure enough, it seems the person who named it also thought it resembled a chrysanthemum. I translated the full name, and it's something like "chrysanthemum-leaved *Eucrypta*" (with *folia* meaning "leaf"). It's native to this area and spreads from the coast to the mountains. I had put the leaves I picked in a cup of water. I was drinking water out of a different cup at the time, and mistakenly drank from the cup with the leaves in it. It had a delicate fragrance, like lemon. The fact that it wasn't just cute but also smelled nice made my heart flutter.

The name "eucrypta" somehow resembles "eucalyptus." The "eu" at the beginning of each name apparently means "well." However, the "crypta" in "eucrypta" means "to hide." The "calyptus" in "eucalyptus" means "to cover" or "be covered." Now, it's not like I'm explaining this to you because I already knew it. I'm just regurgitating the information I found. I'm not at all confident about it. I've never been able to distinguish between the letter "L" and the letter "R," so in this case, I can't be sure whether the meanings are the same or not. I don't even know from what language the names come in the first place. "Eu" looks like it has a Greek origin, but I can't read the Greek alphabet, so I can't look it up on my own. The common English name for eucypta is "hideseed," but I've never once seen anything like a "hidden seed."

Ahh, I searched and searched, but it was just a bunch of stuff I didn't understand. I felt as if I were falling into an oblivion of words. I was also falling into a plant-filled oblivion. Looking for information on weeds is always a matter of life or death.

I had the same feeling several years back, when I searched for and found information on *Zeltnera venusta*, of the Gentiaceae family. Its English name is California centaury. It's the last flower to bloom every year, late in spring, long after all the other flowers. They're the ones with yellow stamens and five-petaled flowers that are bright pink in color and boldly stand out. They all bloom at the same time. And once they stop blooming, springtime in the wasteland comes to an end. It took years for me to determine that this flower was related to the Japanese green gentian.

The name "centaury" apparently comes from the word "centaur." The centaur Chiron was knowledgeable about medicinal plants. In other words, California centaury and the species related to it were all used as medicinal plants. This pink gentian can seemingly be used to treat diarrhea and stomachaches, but I've never tried it myself.

The name *Zeltnera venusta* means "Graceful *Zeltnera*," but no matter how hard I looked through etymology dictionaries, I couldn't figure out what that crucial word "*Zeltnera*" meant. Fully puzzled, I discovered that it was a combination of two European names that belonged to two botanists who had put great effort into studying the plant. It wasn't something that would have shown up in an etymology dictionary.

Not knowing a plant's name. Not even knowing its scientific name. Believing a plant to have a certain scientific name only to have it be replaced by another scientific name that sounds nothing like anything you've ever heard before (as I've recounted in the previous pages here). You struggle and finally determine the common and scientific name of a plant, but it keeps changing minute by minute based on subtle differences you notice. On top of which, you don't get a sense of individuality from the plant. There are so many plants that are more an agglomeration than anything that can be counted one by one, the type of plants that can only be referred to as a "thicket" or a "bush." The more you want to know about a plant's way of life, about its very existence, the more ambiguous it becomes.

I had thought that for humans, there was only one type of existence. Even as I moved to a different country, I still believed this. If I was "Itō Hiromi" in Japan, then I would be "Itō Hiromi" in the United States as well, or worst-case scenario, I would be "Hiromi Ito." But lately I've been thinking that maybe it might be okay not to have such a unified existence. That maybe it's fine if the Japanese Itō and the American Ito are two different people.

If I feel uneasy about living a life where I don't know the names and personalities of plants, well then, what about animals? Animals supposedly live together without any understanding of one another, but is this really the case? With my husband, I only understood one thing—when we have sex, I get pregnant. With my children, the only thing I understood was that when they grow up, they will move away and live a different life. Besides that, I honestly don't understand anything about their feelings or thoughts. Even my dog, whom I raised from a puppy, who relied on me and never left my side and supposedly understood nothing at all—I wasn't able to share any of their feelings of pain or suffering. Without being able to share these feelings, my dog grew old and passed away.

COVERED IN GRASS, I SLEPT

There's this plant called the tumbleweed. It's often tumbling around in the background of Westerns, behind men staring each other down with guns at the ready, or in front of trains heading off into the distance. All the while getting stuck in fences surrounding ranchland. Tumbling through the dusty wasteland, down the solitary road that runs through the wasteland, with no goal whatsoever.

Standing human-like, all alone. Casting a shadow. Casting a shadow, the excessive loneliness of being there grows even stronger.

In the middle of April, I headed north on Interstate Highway 5 and drove for seven hours. Then I drove for seven hours south to return home. I saw tumbleweeds all along the way. Here and there, I saw all kinds of tumbleweeds, both big and small, caught up in fences.

They were more like pieces of trash than they were plants. The kind of trash that washes up with the tide. Like someone had swept up and consolidated dried branches. They seemed to be completely devoid of any kind of life. As if they had been separated from all things necessary to be living beings, including life itself.

They seemed desolate, brutal. It was intense. Naturally, such things didn't tumble around our neighborhood or the nearby park or the residential mall, all of which were meant to be family oriented. It was always on roads that they tumbled. Hit by cars, they smashed to pieces and scattered into the air. They got stuck in the railing along the highway and drifted off toward the roots of trees.

They tumbled up to the top of mountains covered in dried grass and tumbled atop fields of green.

The tumbleweed is an object which cannot be called a plant. This is because they are not alive, and they are all dried out. And yet in this we find the cosmic law of plants in motion. As a result of many years of observation, I have discovered the cosmic law of plants: "'Dying' is 'Living,' and 'Living' is 'Not Dying.'" Although not alive, tumbleweeds move and turn and spread their seeds about. Spreading seed comes from the plant's own volition, but movement comes from the wind. Blown by the wind, plants simply tumble on.

Wind howled through the prairie. Here and there stood pillars of dust. Now and then a large wind came blowing through and rolled up the sand. Aside from the dust and sand, I couldn't see a thing.

Along the side of the road, grasses of the Poaceae family swayed and shook almost as if the wind was trying to break their necks. A tumbleweed blew right by, exuding a devil-may-care attitude.

Tumbleweeds can have one of many different origins. There appear to be many varieties of plants that wither, dry out, detach from their roots, and then take off tumbling. But the best-known one is *Salsola tragus* (otherwise known as *Kali tragus*).

It's not native to the United States. It came mixed into grains that were imported from Russia. It was first reported in South Dakota in 1877. Inland Russia is a flat area prone to drought and covered in grasses that are suited to horse breeding and the cultivation of barley. There, the grasses got blown by the wind and tumbled and tumbled, releasing their seeds as they went. They crossed the sea and ended up arriving at a place also covered in plains. The plains of America, flat and prone to drought, and covered in thickets of sage and grasses of the Poaceae family.

What they met there were stagecoaches, gunmen, Native Americans, bounty hunters, homeless wanderers, gamblers, and all kinds of drifters.

The grasses gradually grew closer to this kind of existence. Human life and grass life crossed over into each other. You could hear the grass breathing. You could also hear the breathing of those people who grew tired of walking, who lay asleep, covered in grass (here I'm borrowing the voice of Takada Ren, who sings a song with similar words written by Okinawan poet Yamanokuchi Baku).

All those people that were called "hobos," that group of vagrants that appeared in America at the beginning of the twentieth century. All those people they called "hippies," that group of people living good lives while also protesting in the second half of the twentieth century. They're still around.

You get it by now, don't you? Tumbleweed isn't merely a type of grass. It's a metaphor for these people who lived and died on those plains, blown by the wind. It's a reality, an existence, a fate that you can't run away from. It's a way of life, and a way of death.

The Japanese name for *Salsola tragus* is *Roshia azami*, or "Russian thistle." And if you write it in Chinese characters, it means "tumbling mugwort." But in no way is it a thistle or mugwort, both of which belong to the Asterceae family. It belongs to the Chenopodiaceae family. Oops, sorry, that's confusing. By calling it an Chenopodiaceae, I'm not really telling it like it is. I had believed it was a Chenopodiaceae for decades, but that family was eliminated with the new APG system of categorization, and it became a member of the Amaranthaceae family. What in the world?

I was well-acquainted with the former Chenopodiaceae family. The thistles I'm used to seeing on the roads of Tokyo and Kumamoto once belonged to the Chenopodiaceae family, as did spinach, beets, Swiss chard, belvedere fruit, and quinoa. Saltwort belonged to the Chenopodiaceae family too, and its genus name is even *Salsola*.

Basically, putting aside the way of life and death of those that tumble for a minute, a large quantity of saltwort, which is native to Russia, naturalized to the American Great Plains. And even though you can soak the young sprouts and put soy sauce on them to make them edible, the Americans of that region were used to eating stuff like bacon and biscuits, and so they didn't know this (there is a description in the twenty-second chapter of Steinbeck's *Grapes of Wrath* of fresh biscuits and bacon, their fragrances wafting through the plains).

I read somewhere something along the lines of "the young buds of the tumbleweed are edible. If there is nothing else to eat, cows, sheep, and horses will eat the young sprouts." Tumbleweeds grow without being eaten, grow and fatten up, and when the time comes, they separate from their roots and take off tumbling down the plains.

Well now, let's get back to Highway 5. It runs through the city of Los Angeles, and crosses over the mountains. It turns into a large plain. There are oil refineries. There are fruit trees. There are pastures for cows and sheep. There are places with a massive accumulation of cows. You just pass right through the middle of it all. Exit ramps. Gas stations, motels, fast food. Billboards that tower over the plains. Road signs.

Even on the exit ramps off the highway, in the fences around the gas stations, you find tumbleweeds drifting in the wind and getting stuck. Interstate highways that cross state lines. County roads. Narrow roads. Tumbleweeds tumbled across those roads that crossed. Almond fields. Peach fields. Plum fields. Grape fields. Tumbleweeds tumbled over grape fields. They even drifted and stuck to the roots of peach trees.

When I did this drive several years ago, I saw dried-up trees here and there along the way. It was a cruel sight. A field full of dried-up trees. Had they faced hard times? Had a disease spread through the field? I imagined several possibilities. I thought about it for a few weeks and then figured out the cause: capitalism. Likely the farm had planned on shutting off the water in order to switch out the crop trees. To do so, they first had to make the trees dry out. Had the trees grown old and then decreased their productivity, and were they therefore to be replaced by trees with crops of a higher demand?

When I did the drive again a while later, I saw green trees with red flowers on them. I passed them by and thought, well now, what kind of red were those red flowers?

They weren't the red of peach blossoms. They weren't the red of cherry blossoms. When I think of red, I think of begonias, but of course these flowers weren't that kind of red. They weren't the red of fuchsias. They weren't the red of roses or geraniums. In fact, they weren't the red of any kind of fruiting tree of the Rosaceae family. And then, I remembered. They were the red of pomegranate flowers. You see pomegranate flowers all over Japan during the rainy season. Bending around fences or bumping into them, those red flowers bloom in the rain.

Pomegranates are popular in California right now. They say they're healthy. Probably healthier than peaches or plums. Pomegranate juice is added to all kinds of health food products. They've become more profitable than peaches or plums. And so I figured that they likely cut the water running to the fields that up until now grew peaches and plums, and uprooted those trees in order to turn them into pomegranate fields.

Passing by the pomegranate, peach, and plum fields, next up were orange fields, lemon fields, and nectarine fields. I turned off Highway 5 and onto Highway 580 and headed west. On hill after hill were groups of white wind turbines stretching back as far as I could see. The throng of cars formed a line underneath them and headed west. I reached my destination.

And within a few days, I had forgotten about the kind of life that was pure movement, and about the tumbleweeds, too.

A few days later, I headed back out on the road. I did so to return home. Heading due east for a spell, and then south. Morning light poured in through the passenger side.

Waves of grass billowed in the morning light on hillside slopes. They billowed on every slope. Billowing, the grass sparkled and then darkened. I thought maybe clouds were moving overhead, casting shadows down below, but there was not a cloud in the sky. Just a solid blue sky. Then I understood it was because of the wind. I understood that the wind moved the blades of grass, and some blades jostled other blades, and they all jostled each other, and all at once they faced the same way and rose up in the same direction.

Like mammals that live in packs, or swarms of insects, or schools of fish, these grasses had formed groups and rose up together in a hurry. Just like how fish flutter their fins and scales to move, grass flaps in the wind and the color of the wave they create changes. That's because each one has a colored tip, white or purple or the like. The waves of grass rose up with a multicolored undulation. The cows, sheep, and horses did not move. The animals didn't move. The grasses rose up in a hurry. A large tumbleweed tumbled out before my eyes. I avoided hitting it, but the truck behind me did not. It was smashed into a million pieces by the truck's large tires, and the image of it scattering into the wind was reflected in my rearview mirror. In an instant, it grew smaller and receded into the distance.

The wasteland stretched out to the left and to the right. A solitary cow lumbered along. I thought maybe it had wandered off from its pack, and then I saw a group of cows further up. The group wasn't moving. Only that one cow was moving, ever so slowly. All that grew in the wasteland were thickets of gray-green sage and tumbleweeds dried black.

Clouds appeared as I was crossing the mountains. There were bushes clumping together along the slopes. There were bushes with blooming yellow flowers. They rustled and looked as if they might get plucked right up. The shadows of the clouds moved along the slopes. Waves of grass rose up whizzing along the slopes, and then fell back down.

The last of the chatty women excused herself and left. While chatting, she had shown off the scar on her waist, which was from surgery and was also the reason she was here soaking in the hot spring water. I told her to take care of herself and realized that only my friend and I remained in the bath. Waterlogged and overheated, we both sat on the edge of the cliffside tub, lazily exposing our naked bodies to the elements. These hot springs, which are located in Minami Aso, are different from the fancy ones you find elsewhere in traditional Japanese inns. There is a health resort attached that has remained unchanged since long ago. Long-term guests can cook their own meals and soak in the waters. While we were there, we could see that kind of atmosphere wafting through the place, even amidst the smell of sulphur, and everyone, including the group of four from Osaka and the three sisters who were visiting from a neighboring prefecture, opened up right away and talked frankly about their travels and injuries and health issues.

The friend accompanying me was an author. I was writing a series of blog posts for her website. I was closer to her than anyone else I knew in my profession, but outside of work, we rarely saw one another. And even though she was more like a colleague, or even a landlord, than a friend, there we were, standing in the changing room, taking off all our clothes, exposing our bodies without shame; soaking in the water until waterlogged and overheated; crawling out into the open air; sitting cross-legged in the buff and chatting away. We didn't care if anyone could see our pubic hair or anything else for that matter.

Directly above us, a Japanese snowbell stood covered in white flowers. The weight of its downward-facing flowers made its branches droop down as if they were soaking in the tub as well. Across the way, the trees that formed a staircase-like pattern along the mountainside bloomed white flowers on their dense branches.

It was then that I heard the following from my friend.

It's written in some book that although the name *unohana* in Japanese refers to the flower we call *utsugi* (or *deutzia* in Latin), it seems that long ago, people used to call any small white flowers that clustered together in bloom around this time of year "*unohana*." Japanese snowbells, the dogwoods that line mountain sides, the *utsugi* along the road, multiflora roses, flowering berries—if it had small white flowers that bloomed in clusters, they called it *unohana*. This is what she explained to me.

I asked her in what book she saw this, but she told me that it was a story she heard from someone long ago, and so she didn't have any source for it. All the same, I felt her story was true. But not just that—it also made me feel a certain nostalgia. The story moved me, and I felt like I had been waiting to hear such a story for a long time.

For a long time, I was unable to figure out the true essence of this flower we call *unohana*. I first tried looking up a song I had learned in elementary school that mentioned a "hedge that smelled of *unohana*." I knew it was another name for *utsugi*, but I had never seen *utsugi* along the back alleys of Tokyo, and if they had grown there, no one had pointed them out to me as a child saying "ah, that's *utsugi*." The song also mentioned the *hototogisu* (or "lesser cuckoo" in English), but I had never seen one of these either, and I mistakenly thought the song referred to its "quiet *sleeping*" when in fact it referred to its "quiet *weeping*." I was shocked when my mother brought a dish made of soy pulp home from the tofu shop and called it "*unohana*." In high school and in college, I would read something about *unohana* and get interested and look it up, but each time I would end up not being able to differentiate it from *utsugi*.

And so we left the water and got dressed, and headed toward the airport along a mountain road, the strong smell of sulphur wafting all the while. There were fully-grown Japanese snowbells. White flowers bloomed and fell to the ground. Along the roadside grew stalks of *mamushigusa* (or jack-in-the-pulpit) blooming blue-black flowers. Saxifrages of all shapes bloomed white flowers. The roadside was overflowing with roses that wriggled and bloomed white flowers. White. They were all white. Like white rabbits flocking together—*unohana*.

Among all of these, one flower stood out. A shrub, with tightly packed flowers that faced downward. The petals were split in half, white on this side and rouge on the other. That was the impression I got. We should have pulled the car over so that I could pick one and look at it, but since we didn't, all I can say is, "that was the impression I got."

The fog rolled in. Something jumped out right in front of us. It was a monkey. A monkey walked out step by step by step onto the road and stood there, and then nimbly jumped into the thicket on the side of the road. Jumping, it made the branches in the thicket come to life. A monkey. I had heard that they lived around here, but I had never expected to see one. It was completely different from seeing a fox or a *tanuki*, a racoon dog. It stood in the road and stared right into my eyes. It stared unblinkingly.

The fog rapidly grew denser. We couldn't even see ten meters ahead of us. Rounding a curve, a cow suddenly appeared out of nowhere. All of a sudden there were hazard lights lit up ahead of us. As we got closer, we saw a large bus that was stopped and blocking part of the road. People wearing mountain climbing equipment shuffled around the sides of the bus.

"Don't rush, go slowly, go slowly," my friend cried out again and again from the passenger seat.

The fog grew even denser. Now five meters ahead was covered in fog. We drove and drove but couldn't seem to get to the airport. The car's navigation system calmly recalculated our path and continued to point the way.

Crossing over the mountain, the road turned into a long downward slope. At last, the fog cleared. We could no longer see the clumps of small white flowers. Bead trees bloomed in their place. We could see an ambiguous color along the canopies of the groves here and there, and it was hard to determine if the color was grey or purple. It looked like mist, but it was actually clusters of flowers on the bead trees. I told my friend that with a single step into the grove, one would be surrounded by its fragrance. But, I also told her, because the flowers are up so high on the trees, one wouldn't really be able to see them.

My friend told me there are bead trees in Tateyama and certain parts of Tokyo, but the ones in Tateyama are in a garden. That bead trees grew in parts of Hakone, and the ones there didn't look like garden trees—so perhaps Hakone was the northernmost limit for them.

Flowers referred to as "*utsugi*" extend over a variety of taxonomical families. The principal one is the Saxifragaceae family, but there is also the Caprifoliaceae family and the Rosaceae family. If it is a shrub that has small white flowers that bloom in clusters around this time of year, then it is an *utsugi*.

Looking up the Saxifragaceae family—which is the family that includes hydrangeas in addition to *utsugi*—I learned that it, too, like the Liliaceae family, met its sorrowful downfall with the change in the system of categorization. Both hydrangeas and *utsugi* now belong to the Hydrangeaceae family. Truly, all things must pass.

No matter how much I searched, I couldn't find a photo that matched those white and rouge flowers. I should have focused my eyes on their color and shape, taken them in wide eyed, pulled over the car and gotten close to them, taken them in my hands and stared at them hard, but now I can't recall the fine details of their appearance, no matter how I try. It fills me with regret. Everything remains as it was, covered in fog. Maybe it belonged to the honeysuckle family, maybe a *Weigela coraeensis* or a *Weigela decora*—just as I became aimlessly lost in anguish circling around the area in my mind, I suddenly hit upon the idea of going to the Kenmotsudai Arboretum located at Kumamoto Castle. I thought maybe it was growing there, that maybe someone there would know what it was.

The Kenmotsudai Arboretum sits at the northern edge of the castle grounds. The castle's small garden, which is lined with cherry and camphor trees, has been there since long ago. I rode my bike to the parking lot at the southern edge of the castle's grounds and cut through the plaza of the outer citadel on my way to the arboretum. I went this way because I wanted to see the large camphor trees that dot the plaza grounds. They all stood silently luxuriant. There are plenty of large camphors in the area. At the west edge of the castle grounds, there are seven of them growing together that are between one hundred and a thousand years old.

At the information desk, I made an appeal to someone who looked more official than a botanist: "On the mountain road in Minami Aso, I saw these flowers that were two-toned in color ..." They seemed to know what I was talking about: "Ahh.... I wonder if it's that one flower, this one here, this one." They pulled out a field guide and pointed to the one they meant and called out to someone working outdoors that looked more like a gardener than a botanist, who climbed down a ladder and came in drying off their hands and said, "Ahh, that's a *Weigela decora*."

Weigela decora was included in the field guide that the official-looking person pulled out, but the rouge color I had seen was not. That color that I saw just wouldn't reappear in any picture whatsoever. I had no choice but to give up.

If you leave the Kenmostudai Arboretum and go down the sudden slope next to the castle, and keep going down and down and down, you'll end up around where my house is. Right in front of it flows the Tsuboi River, which in turn flows into the castle moat. Someone told me recently that long ago, row houses belonging to low-ranking samurai used to stretch out around here. It was surely that kind of place—damp, sure to flood with each heavy rainfall; where mosquitos endlessly well up throughout the long, hard summers; where the sky above the riverbank stretches out wide, but where everything else feels cramped and one must go on living aware of the fact that they are always being watched by others.

Because it floods with each big rainfall, about twenty years ago, the prefectural government tore up the whole region and created flood gates, building up the embankments and closing in the wetlands. As the heavy rains continue and the water level in the river rises, the prefecture opens the flood gates and lets the water enter the embankments. Both sides of the embankment become submerged underwater. The flood warning siren cries out sharp and low in the rain throughout the whole region—it's a terribly ominous sound. When the water recedes, the embankments turn to wetlands as far as the eye can see, and the daisies and wild grasses grow rampant, now as they did long ago.

Right after all this work had been done to build the flood gates, bead trees began to grow in the wetlands. At first, they were small, frail little trees. They quickly grew and flourished, and bloomed flowers and produced seeds. They grew up and created shade for herons and pheasants. They grew that much in twenty-years' time.

Once I knew how to spot a bead tree, I noticed them here and there. Not so much the ones in gardens, but wild ones that bloom in May. As I stand on the low ground along the river and look up at the high ground that surrounds me, I see that all the forests are dense with trees. Each forest is covered in a haze of bead tree blossoms.

Although so many grow in the village, I didn't see any bead trees in the mountains. All I noticed were the *unohana* and that red-white *utsugi*. That's why *utsugi* was all I could think about. But once I came down from the mountain, my eye turned from the *utsugi* to the bead tree, and there was nothing I could do about it.

As for that thing I saw on the mountain, I came upon the name *tsukushiyabu-utsugi* while I was searching for what it could be. I read that it's unique to the low-mountain areas of Kyushu and has downward-facing flowers, just like the ones I saw. But on a different website it said that it's difficult to differentiate between the *tsukushiyabu-utsugi*, the *tani-utsugi*, and the *hakone-utsugi* because they are all similar species and there are many natural hybrids. It was right around then that I called off my investigation. I was fine with this flower being "a certain" *utsugi* of the honeysuckle family. It wasn't an *unohana*, but it was a variety of *utsugi* that bloomed in clumps, and I was fine with that.

I left California, with its fresh-feeling, perpetual spring weather, and wandered around Narita Airport, then Haneda Airport, and then arrived in Kumamoto. Outside of the air-conditioned airport, it was the rainy season. My body wasn't used to it, and for the first day or two I had the sensation that droplets of water were clinging to all my pores. Feeling that way, I walked around the city—or maybe I should say I swam around it. The trees and grasses were uncountable, immeasurable in their existence. Droplets of water found their way into the moss growing on the stone wall outside Kumamoto Castle, and had turned the moss soft, like jelly, seeping out of every crevice in the wall. My pores felt just like that, unable to endure the water, sucking it all up and then spilling it back out. But that unpleasant feeling really only lasted a day or two, and then my skin remembered this kind of climate and began breathing in the humidity with all its might.

It was some ten years or so ago, but I used to live a life in which I would return here every summer and give my daughter a ride on my bike to and from the preschool on the other side of the river.

Way back when, the whole area was wetlands. It was twenty years ago that they built embankments around the circumference of the wetlands and created both a man-made pond in the center to prevent flooding and flood gates to help manage the water. The road atop the embankment was a bumpy one, and it was difficult to ride your bike on. Compared to the lower road, which saw a lot more traffic, the grass on the upper road was flourishing, and there was more water running through it. There were all kinds of things living there, which made it fun.

I would pull my bike along and walk my daughter up the embankment. When we'd reach the road atop the embankment, I would put her in the child seat and slowly start pedaling. We'd follow the road atop the embankment and circle around the riverbank. *Seibanmorokoshi* (Johnson grass) would lean in from both sides of the road. Kudzu would stretch out its tendrils.

My daughter was five or six years old. She'd say, "I wanna get down, I wanna get down," and I would stop the bike. On one such occasion, she quickly got out of the child seat, stood on one foot, and extended both arms out and then brought them together right in front of her face. A blue heron stood in the river, making the same pose.

When we would pass by some sunflowers, the child would open her eyes wide and purse her lips. She said that this was the expression sunflowers made. One day, we saw that the sunflowers had all at once withered and drooped their necks. And so my daughter, too, drooped her neck and hung her head low.

But it was the kudzu that was really interesting. From across the way, it stretched out its tendrils incessantly, trying to touch us. Every time we rode the bike along the narrow road that ran atop the embankment of the riverbank, we couldn't help but trample on the tips of the kudzu tendrils. They crawled out into the places that we couldn't avoid trampling. At first, we avoided them, but soon we discovered that we were simply unable to do so. We also discovered that the kudzu didn't mind being trampled on. If we crushed it in the morning, by evening it would double in size, and the tip of the vine that had been trampled would pretty much return to its original state. And with a dogged perseverance, it would continue to stretch out.

Every time the bike would trample over a kudzu vine, my daughter would scream. And then she would laugh, as if someone were tickling her. And then I would call out, saying, "Kudzu-san, I'm sorry! I'm sorry Kudzu-san!" As I said this, we'd keep on trampling it.

The tips of the vines were covered in fuzz, like puppies, and would sway back and forth, and even though vines *should* crawl along the ground, these would stand erect and move in close. They really seemed as if they were full of desire. My daughter was small, so she was able to laugh at them, but if I had been accompanied by a young girl that had already gone through puberty, I would have tactfully tried to ignore the vines' shamelessness, their salaciousness.

Around that time, a terrible incident occurred on the road atop the embankment. In the early morning, a young woman who was riding her bike along the road was raped. A man hid in the thicket and went after the woman as she passed by. My house is part of a housing complex built on the embankment. You can look down from the upper floor and see the whole riverbank. Several residents of the complex said they heard a high, thin voice. They had thought it was a bird and said that they couldn't believe such a thing could have occurred where it did. The thicket was comprised mostly of *seibanmorokoshi* and *seitaka-awadachisō*. *Seibanmorokoshi* was clumped together along the edge of the road. A little bit further back, *seitaka-awadachisō* clustered together. It was still young and stiff. Underneath it were old stumps of mugwort, entangled in Japanese hops and *yabugarashi*, or "bushkiller" in English.

After the incident, the men who lived in our housing complex came shuffling out and began periodically cutting down and removing all of the *seibanmorokoshi*. They said they couldn't wait on the city or the prefecture to periodically cut it. This way, at least, the area where the man who attacked the woman had hidden would be regularly rendered naked, and no man could hide himself there.

Within less than a week, the mowed-down *seibamorokoshi* had re-grown to its original condition.

They caught the man who did it. But I couldn't help thinking that it was the kudzu that had done it. Every morning, before my very eyes, I had seen the tips of the hairy kudzu buds stretch out and come crawling along the ground, looking for a way to touch us. The vines we crushed in the morning lay as they were, and stood back up erect in the evening, swaying their stems and moving in on women—I had seen this, as well.

They were more like snakes than plants. Even more than snakes, they resembled those eels that sway in the ocean. There are stories in old books about snakes that enter women's bedchambers at night, and one about a snake that slid into a woman's vagina after she had climbed a tree. Couldn't all these stories be about kudzu? The tips of their stems are hidden in fuzz, but you can imagine that hidden under that hair are teeth or a penis.

Of course, I didn't mention any of this to my daughter. To her, "Kudzu-san" was a fun plant to play with. And so, with each trampling of its tendril tips, we'd apologize to Kudzu-san. Now she's a high schooler, and her Japanese and her emotional disposition have not matured to the level that her body has, and when we go back to Kumamoto, she looks at the kudzu nostalgically, as if she were visiting an older family friend that had played with her as a child. She seems to want to call out: "Kudzu-san! Kudzu-san!"

Now, I have in front of me a book called *Rural Plants of Southern Kyushu*. It was published in June of 2001. I bought it around that time. I crisscrossed the Pacific Ocean with this book in my arms. I brought it back to California and read it there, and in that dry, monotonous climate I dreamed of those evergreen forests and multicolored naturalized plants of Southern Kyushu that seem to have trouble breathing in the thick air. Whenever I come back to

Kumamoto, I of course have to bring the book with me. When I looked kudzu up in the book, I found it right there in the opening pages. I wondered, "Why the special treatment?" But as I opened to it, I realized why. It's one of the so-called "seven autumnal flowers." The book begins with the traditional seven flowers of spring, and then the seven flowers of autumn, and is then divided into plants of the roadside, the fields and wetlands, the sandy coastline, and the low mountains. I had forgotten all about the fact that kudzu was one of the seven autumnal flowers, because at the time I was only preoccupied with its ability to grow on and on without a care in the world. Kudzu was a common, useful plant. Its leaves provided food for horses and cows; its vines were woven into baskets and twisted into rope, and was even tuned into cloth as well. Its roots were used as medicine and also used to make a healthy starch. On top of which, it had pretty flowers, if you looked close enough.

Its overpowering vitality was likely the same long ago as it is today, and I imagine that back then it climbed up trees and wrapped around them and squirmed through fields and continued growing until there was nothing to be seen but kudzu.

I suddenly decided to search for poems about kudzu in the *Man'yōshu*, Japan's oldest extent collection of poetry, from the eighth century. These days, you can easily (too easily, with no thrill of the hunt) find such things by searching for the words "*Man'yōshu*, kudzu." I found many poems. I picked two or three that struck my fancy and tried translating them word-for-word into modern Japanese.

The first poem meant something like this: "Because no news arrives of you, you who have been as constant as the summer kudzu, I cannot help worrying that something has happened."

The next one meant something like: "Deep in worry like a summer field covered in kudzu, what has become of my life?"

The third one meant: "There is no field of kudzu that a horse cannot cross. What is with this gossip? Come meet me and say it to my face."

I figured that since I found these in the *Man'yōshu*, I should be able to find kudzu in Japan's earliest mytho-historical text, the *Ko-jiki*, which also dates back to the eighth century, but I couldn't find any. Vines appear frequently throughout it. For example, when the creator god Izanagi returns from the underworld, what he throws at his pursuers is a vine called "*kuromi-kazura*," and this then grows into a vine called "*ebi-kazura*." Both have the word "*kazura*" in their name, a word which means "vine," so I thought maybe they were kudzu. But they weren't. If these had been kudzu, they would've immediately run rampant, with such intensity one would think they were trying to work up a sweat, and thwarted the pursuers by preventing them from advancing.

However, by the time we reach the tenth-century poetry collection the *Kokinshū*, kudzu becomes weakened to a shocking degree, possessing only two set images: that of "changing colors in the autumn" and "being blown by the wind and turning one's back (in resentment)." The kudzu that grew so dense it worked up a sweat is nowhere to be found. Take, for example, the following poems:

> Even the kudzu that crawls
> along the fence
> within the shrine
> cannot withstand the autumn
> and has changed color

> Just as the autumn wind blows
> turning the kudzu leaves so that their backs show,
> seeing you turn your back to me
> in resentment
> —Oh, how bitter it makes me feel

And the same is true for the eleventh-century *The Tale of Genji*. For example, there is a poem in the chapter "Spring Shoots" that mentions how "the kudzu that crawls on the shrine fence has changed its color," and one in the chapter "Evening Mist" that mentions the "treetops and leaves of the kudzu on the peak that cannot endure the mountain gales." There's also one in the chapter "Trefoil Knots" that reads:

> Oh the kudzu
> that climbs so patiently
> on that stone fence in the mountain village
> where that someone I once knew
> is no more

Ever since the *Kokinshū*, kudzu has become a stock image in this way, and even when such poems use the word "kudzu," there is the possibility that they are actually talking about a different plant altogether. To explain why, let's take a look at the following section from the *Tale of Genji* chapter "Evening Faces:"

> A bright green vine, its white flowers smiling to themselves,
> was clambering merrily over what looked like a board fence.[3]

The original Japanese uses the word "kudzu" to mean "vine" here, but it is actually describing the *yūgao* or "evening face" vine (which has the scientific name *Lagenaria siceraria var. hispida*). Kudzu flowers are not white. *The Tale of Genji* was written by the eminent Murasaki Shikibu, who came long before I did and whose writing ability I normally greatly respect—but when it comes to kudzu, she had absolutely no interest in the plant, and displayed no interest in paying any attention to it.

Moving through the ages, we have *sekkyōbushi*, which are oral narratives meant to illustrate Buddhist teachings from the beginning of the medieval period. In the *sekkyōbushi* titled *Shinoda-zuma*, there is a heroine named "Kuzu-no-ha," or "Kudzu Leaf."

She is originally a fox, but she transforms into a human woman and becomes the wife of a man named Abe-no-Yasuna. She gives birth to a child named Abe-no-Seimei (who becomes a legendary astrologer in the *onmyōji* tradition). Eventually, her true form is revealed, and she returns to the forest in tears, leaving behind this poem:

> If you feel lonely
> Come and visit
> The forest of Shinoda known as Izumi
> Where thoughts of you come back every time the wind blows
> Through these kudzu leaves

Here again we see the post-*Kokinshū* trope of kudzu leaves showing their backsides when blown by the wind, but the poem perfectly overlays the reality of the kudzu leaves with the reality of the woman, and it is heartbreaking. I may well know this experience in my own body.

You can find variations on the "fox wife" tale here and there. Usually, she ends up having her original form revealed and returning to the forest. There is one in the *Nihon Ryōiki*, which is a collection of folklore from the early Heian period dating to sometime between the end of the eighth century and the beginning of the ninth century, that claims the word for fox, *kitsune*, can be traced back to a pun originating from this tale. But in that version, kudzu in its actual plant form is nowhere to be found.

In the United States, kudzu is an invasive species that has become uncontrollable. It was imported first as an ornamental plant for flower gardens, and would later be used as feed for livestock. People who have been to the American South say that it is lousy with kudzu, but I've never seen it once in California. Maybe because the climate is too dry, or maybe because there are many Japanese immigrants that know better than to do something as reckless as plant kudzu.

And then the rain stopped. I climbed the embankment, hoping to see some kudzu. My daughter is no longer here, and neither is my father. I no longer follow the road atop the embankment to reach the preschool or visit my father's house. The rain that had just been falling had pooled on this road atop the embankment, making it muddy. I got stuck in the mud, I slipped in the mud. I had no choice but to walk on the grass along the roadside.

Of course, kudzu was squirming all over the riverbank. But it had just started growing. It hadn't yet reached the apex of its vitality, its sexual desire. Before long, it started raining again. The cloudy sky, it hung low, somehow holding back, trying to hold on to the rain drops. But it appeared as if, eventually, rain would come spilling out from between its fingers in any case. And now, each plant sucks that moisture up with its whole body. It accumulates there, in the body, readying to explode.

AREXA KAWARANSIS

When I think about it, up until now I've written an awful lot about plants. Ever since I first started writing poetry, I've been repeating the names of naturalized plants like *Conyza sumatrensis* and *Solidago altissima*. This has been at the root of my poetry.

Naturalized plants covered everything. They grew along the roadsides of the back streets of northern Tokyo, where I grew up, and in the empty lots here and there, and on the riverbank of the Arakawa. The riverbank was too far for a child's feet to reach, and I would get exhausted just getting there. It wasn't the kind of place where you could go play every day. It was a big river, spanned by an iron bridge that let off a thunderous roar. I never even considered crossing over to the other side. Along the riverbank was a crematorium for humans, and one for animals. There was also a place that dealt with placentas. In my child's mind, I would think: "This is the boundary, I am at the boundary."

Both *Conyza sumatrensis* and *Solidago altissima* grew thick and dense around there. If you stepped into the thickets, it was unbearably muddy, and there was garbage that had been thrown around. There were pools of oil and carcasses of dead animals. Had they died there, or been thrown there after they died? Since I was only a child, I was unable to tell. It was just . . . just that . . . I had the feeling that they had been brought even further over to the other side of the boundary, and it was terrifying. And so, the other children and I stepped gently into the thicket and got all muddy and covered in oil. When we stepped on a corpse, we would scream as loud as we could.

There's a game called *engacho* that we all loved playing at the time. Actually, no, we didn't love it. We hated it, but we felt we had to play it to stay alive. If we came across something unclean or impure, we would say the word "*gacho*" to ward off defilement. It was that simple of a game. Thus we began playing *engacho* over and over again from the minute that we stepped into the riverbank. We felt we couldn't stop playing it.

It was the boundary. The boundary was thoroughly impure. The naturalized plants that grew so thickly there had, by themselves, crossed over the boundary and settled there.

For me, growing up was an experience spent writhing around in pain. But somehow or other I did grow up and become an adult. And then I migrated to Kumamoto and began taking walks around the riverbank of the Tsuboi. I found there a type of grass I didn't recognize. It was a tall grass with small purple flowers that bloomed in clusters. It grew all over and bloomed all over. Up close, the small flowers were beautiful. But the overall impression they gave off was more brutal than beautiful.

So I pulled out an illustrated field guide of plants and looked the grass up. It was a guide meant for adults that I had purchased near the end of my teenage years. At that time, I used it over and over to look up naturalized plants. Most of them were of the Asteraceae family. They grew thick and dense on the riverbank. I discovered their names one by one. That was the guidebook I used.

The grass I hadn't recognized wasn't in the guidebook. I checked many other books too, but I couldn't find it. I thought it resembled a type of verbena called seashore vervain. I also thought it resembled one called purpletop vervain. But they were each subtly different from the one I was looking for. I went a long time without knowing what it was. Then one day a friend of mine who was born in

America but had been living in Japan for decades (but couldn't speak Japanese) taught me what it was. "That's Brazilian vervain," he said. Of all the ways to learn this, to be taught about a naturalized plant by a human who was himself much like a naturalized plant ... I murmured to myself, "Eh, I've lost my touch," but by then, the internet was already a thing, and I was able to successfully look it up.

I learned that Brazilian vervain was a newly naturalized plant. Of the Verbenaceae family, it was first identified around 1957 in Ōmuta, and then it spread all over Kyushu, and then all over the whole of Western Japan. Then I understood: It wasn't something I could have seen growing up in Tokyo when I did. It was something that wouldn't have been included in a botanical field guide published in the 1970s. In the meantime, it continued to spread like this along the riverbanks of Kumamoto.

While thinking too much about naturalized plants, I had a moment where I couldn't tell if I, myself, were a human being or if I were a plant. It happened when I was writing a long-form poem titled *Wild Grass on the Riverbank*. And while I find it tactless to discuss my own poetry, now that I am discussing plants, I really want to talk about it.

It's a long-form poem that I began writing around the summer of 2004 and finished up at the end of 2005. But for many years before that I had been dashing off rough drafts. I was thinking that I wanted to introduce narrative into modern poetry, much like epic poetry or the oral storytelling of *sekkyōbushi*. Therefore, there is a narrative story in *Wild Grass on the Riverbank*.

There's a mother and two children. The older sister is named Natsukusa and the younger brother is named Zushio. Of course, the younger brother's name comes from the legend of *Sanshō the Bailiff*. Accompanied by their mother, the two move around here and there. At some point they settle down in the wasteland (a place similar to the brutal wastelands of Southern California). There they get a new father and a new little sister. Before long the father dies and becomes a corpse. Of course, the description of this part comes close to the tale *Oguri Hangan*. From there, the family returns to the riverbank (a place similar to the dense riverbanks of Kumamoto). On the riverbank, where naturalized plants grow rank, another personality appears alongside Natsukusa—one named Alexa. They have their ups and downs on the riverbank, and then Alexa disappears. Like the princess from the *sekkyōbushi* titled *Shintokumaru*, Natsukusa takes her younger siblings and leaves the riverbank to return to the wasteland. Waiting for them is the father who should be dead—but he has instead returned to life and has grown as large as a sequoia tree several thousands of years old.

That's the story. The humans, however, only play supporting roles. The plants are the main characters, in particular the naturalized plants of Japan's riverbanks.

Every summer during the period in which I wrote this poem, I would look out toward the riverbank and watch the *Sorghum halepense*, the *Conyza sumatrensis*, and the *Solidago altissima* rise and fall as they blew in the wind. I thought a lot about them. How could I put them into words? Would I be able to represent their movements, their lifeforce, exactly as I saw them?

> *Sorghum halepense* fell over and got back up
> *Solidago altissima* was still young, its stalk and leaves were green
> It was pushed over by the wind, as if to say, you, get over there,
>   then it pushed the next stalk
> The next stalk too, pushed the next stalk as if to say, you, get over
>   there
> The next stalk after the next stalk also pushed the next stalk as if
>   to say, you, get over there, you, get over there
> You, get over there, *Solidago altissima* was pushed over, you, get
>   over there, was pushed, you, get over there
> You, get over there

The kudzu vines squirmed, grew up
Onto the embankment, stuck out their tips, waited, then grew
    tired[4]

It took several years to write this one verse. All summer long I stared out at the grass and felt that my eyesight had turned strange with the dazzling light it gave off as it swayed. In the 1960s there was this thing called "op art," associated with artists like Bridget Riley, and looking at the grass felt like I was looking at that sort of thing. I tried writing about it in a number of different ways. None of them went well, and during the same season of the following year, I once again stared out at the grass. But I couldn't capture it in writing, and so once again the following year ... I repeated this cycle again and again. Year after year I gazed out to the place where the *Solidago altissima* shook in the wind. And then one year I was finally able to write it. To write it just as I saw it. An emotion that exceeded the feeling of a Bridget Riley painting, something like malice, came out on the surface of it. I don't know why it turned out this way, when I was intentionally trying to push emotion aside.

The English translation of *Wild Grass on the Riverbank* is by Jeffrey Angles. I could not have higher confidence in his translation. The style of translation is almost like a possession—to a frightening degree. It doesn't really use any words that I am unfamiliar with. The poem is composed only of words that would not seem strange coming from my own mouth. But naturally the English is not the type of English I speak, which is a type based on Japanese. It's a much smoother representation.

It's been twenty years since I began living with English. While I still cannot read or write it comfortably, I can understand most things in spoken speech, and I can express some complex ideas. I can express them, but my accent is strong. It's to the point that if someone were standing thirty meters away and heard me say one word, they would know I'm Japanese. In Japanese I can read, write, speak loudly, and whisper with complete control, and so my frustration with English knows no bounds. But that's how I live.

The first-person subject in the poem is Natsukusa. Long ago, when I wrote *Wild Grass on the Riverbank*, Natsukusa used Japanese. But now, through the translation, it is in English that she narrates her feelings and her experiences. But her English resembles my own. When I hear it, I feel overly empathetic and my heart fills up. Sometimes, I find places in the translation that make me think, "So that's what it was," or, "So that's what I was trying to say." It's like a dream. It feels comforting, like something is being cured deep in my subconscious.

Each English expression in the translation looks me in the eyes and confirms: "You've had this kind of experience, and you've had that kind of experience, and this is how you express them in English, and that's how you wanted to express those experiences, right?" But I don't want to agree with this, as I hold within me a feeling that borders on absolute faith when it comes to the Japanese language. But as I read the translation out loud, I begin to have the feeling that maybe I did want to write it in words that were, by and large, not Japanese.

When I read aloud the English used in the translation, I am taken in by the delusion that *this* is my real voice, and that I've always, from the very start, spoken that way. In other words, I can't shake the feeling that the Japanese version of *Wild Grass on the Riverbank* is a mere translation, and that the English version is the original.

There's a passage in the poem that repeats the names of naturalized plants. In Japanese it goes like this:

> *hime, mukashi, yomogi, ō, arechi, nogiku, yabu, karashi,*
> *kana, mugura, seiban, morokoshi, kayatsuri, gishi, gishi, ibo,*
> *kusa, yōshuya, mago, bō, gama, yoshi, ogi, nono, hime, gama,*
> *no, yoshi, nono, ogi, no*

This is based on the following plant names: *himemukashiyomogi, ō-arechinogiku, yabukashira, kanamugura, seibanmorokoshi, kayatsurigusa, gishigishi, ibokusa, yōshuyamagobō, gama, yoshi, ogi,* and *himegama.*

When repeating the names in the poem, I took them apart and broke them up. And I added the sound "*no,*" which can mean "field," as a way to keep time with the rhythm.

In the English translation, the plant names became Latinized. The English names for plants bear traces of people's everyday lives and emotions, like horseweed (which is the English name for *himemukashiyomogi*) or Johnson grass (which is the English name for *seibanmorokoshi*). They are the everyday lives and emotions of strangers, and so I feel no empathy for them.

Ō + arechi + no + giku and *hime + mukashi + yomogi,* I factorized them out in this way. I combined each prime factor and named them like this. I cut them loose from everyday life. I threw emotions away. These were the names I preferred. Accordingly, if a sense of everyday life or emotion should get mixed into these names unexpectedly, then that word's meaning would flare up all of a sudden. Like it does with *arechinogiku* (as "*arechi*" means "wasteland") or *seitaka-awadachisō* (as "*seitaka*" means "tall"). Like *noborogiku* (as "*boro*" means "tattered clothes").

Kawara Arekusa (which is both the name of the poem in Japanese and the full name of the character Alexa within the poem) is of course a fictional name. I wanted to hide her, this girl of the Hominidae family, in the vicinity of plants like *himemukashiyomogi* or *ō-arechinogiku* of the Asteraceae family, or *arechihanagasa* of the Verbenaceae family. And so I've been thinking about it a lot—that I need to give Kawara Arekusa a Latinized name.

When naming something in Latin like "*Something or-other,*" the "*Something*" is the genus name. For the "*or-other*" you put an adjective that is limited to the specific plant you are naming. So something like: *Alexa kawaransis*. No, since it is a Japanese person who cannot differentiate between L and R, perhaps it should be *Arexa kawaransis?*

With a ring to it like "*otakusa,*" as found in *Hydrangea otaksa*, the Latin name for the flower we call *ajisai* in Japanese. An adjective in which the name "Otaki-san" lies hidden—the name of the Japanese woman Philipp Franz von Seabold loved and then left behind.

A DECLARATION OF RELIGIOUS FAITH:
TO ALL THE EX-TAXODIACEAE

In the peak of summer I went to Takachiho in Miyazaki Prefecture, driving from Kumamoto and crossing the southern tip of Aso. I wanted to see *sugi*—the Japanese cedar or *Cryptomeria japonica*. Takachiho is full of *sugi*. No, actually, it's more accurate to say that it's full of *sugi* and full of shrines. No, actually, it's even more accurate to say it's full of *sugi*, shrines, and gorges. Iwato Shrine, on the outskirts of Takachiho, has all three: *sugi*, shrine, and gorge.

Iwato Shrine has an eastern shrine and a western shrine with a gorge running in between. If you make a request at the western shrine, the senior priest will open up the closed gate and escort you inside. Within a stand of trees deep inside there is a designated place for worshiping from a distance, and you can see the gorge from there. You can see the opposite shore. As I regarded how both this side and that side were covered in trees, giving off a luster deep enough to take away one's breath, the priest spoke, saying that the *shintai*, or place in which the *kami* of the shrine resides, is the cave that served as the hiding place for the sun goddess Amaterasu, of a well-known tale from Japan's earliest mythology. He said it was over on the other side of the gorge, but that no one had gone inside for several hundreds of years, and so it was in pretty bad shape.

He said there were seven old *sugi* growing over there, and that it was not a place that people could enter, but that you can see the tops of the trees from where we were. I looked to where he was pointing, and the tops of thick, fluffy trees were sticking out from the top of the forest.

There are *sugi* groves on the slopes of all the mountains of Kumamoto. The *sugi* that were planted there grow uniformly in rows, and it feels like you can almost hear the screeching sound of lines being drawn with a ruler.

Here's an old story. In Kumamoto there were heavy rains that fell before the rainy season began, and they wrecked the mountains. They set the *sugi* groves adrift, and they got stuck and dammed up the rivers, which then flooded. Right after this happened, I went and witnessed the horror. The city of Aso suffered a lot of damage. The ground was mud-colored everywhere, and countless *sugi* were soaking in the river. Their branches were gone, their bark completely peeled off—it was as if they had been polished. They had become "lumber" more so than "trees," and the area was now just like the old-fashioned lumber yards they called "*kiba*." The person who was guiding me at the time said: "These are all plantation *sugi*." Since that moment I had been convinced—baselessly—that since so many of these trees were from tree plantations, that *sugi* must be non-native.

But *sugi* are a native species to Japan. You can find them in the ancient chronicles of the *Kojiki*. The serpent Yamata no Orochi is described in the following manner in the *Kojiki*, and this is the first *sugi* to appear in the Japanese language:

> His eyes are like red ground cherries; his one body has eight heads and eight tails. On his body grow moss and cypress and cryptomeria trees. His length is such that he spans eight valleys and eight mountain peaks. If you look at his belly, you see that blood is oozing out all over it.[5]

The original text was written in kanbun, a modified form of Classical Chinese writing that was used for writing Japanese at the time.

It uses the character 蘿 for "moss," the character 檜 for "cypress," and the character 椙 for "cryptomeria" or *sugi*.

Sugi pollen flew through the air of the ancient past of the *Kojiki*, the *Nihon shoki*, and the *Man'yōshū*. Even if their roots weren't deep, the trees grew, they grew big, they passed through the years, they kept on living for hundreds of years, and were worshipped all over.

But then I realized: I didn't actually know the true nature of *sugi*. I had been familiar with the name "*sugi*" since childhood. I had grown up singing songs about "waking the wild grass called '*sugi no ko*,'" and the one about "opening up the door made of *sugi* in the morning." But I can't tell whether a particular tree is a *sugi* or a *hinoki* cypress. On top of which, I don't have seasonal allergies, and so I don't even notice when their flowers bloom. When I looked it up, the name *sugi* itself was a rather willy-nilly one.

The school song sung at the high school in my hometown, which I sang all the time and still remember, started like this: "A new bud sprouts into a Himalaya *sugi* . . ." There was a large Himalaya *sugi* in the school's courtyard. Unlike the cherry trees or gingkoes that you can find anywhere, this was an evergreen conifer, dignified and Western-looking, like a Christmas tree. I thought in my child's mind (which I say even though I was in high school) that it was cool. But the true nature of Himalaya *sugi*, in fact, is that it is a *sugi* in name only. It is actually of the Pinaceae or pine family. And not just the Himalaya *sugi*, but also the Lebanon *sugi*, which appears often in the Bible. It's false advertising—it, too, is of the Pinaceae family.

The fact that the English name for *sugi* is "Japanese cedar" has been stuck in my head ever since I learned it from a dictionary at the age of twelve or thirteen, when I had just started learning English. However, when I look up "cedar" now, here is what comes up: "A plant of the Pinaceae family and the genus of Himalaya *sugi*."

There is a movie that in Japanese is called *Snow Falling on Himalaya Sugi*. If you were to go into it thinking you'd see a story about the Himalayas, you'd be wrong. The original title of the movie is *Snow Falling on Cedars*, and it's a story about Washington state in the American Northwest, not about the Himalayas. It's a place where Japanese Americans had lived and suffered hardships. Naturally, what grows native there is not Himalaya *sugi*, but rather red cedars. (These are different from redwoods, which I will talk about later.) Again, not *sugi*, but rather trees of the Cupressaceae or cypress family, within the genus *Thuja*. It was a beautiful film. The trees were really beautiful. They were straight and damp, and closely resembled the *sugi* from groves in Japan. Perhaps because *sugi* have been so closely tied to people's everyday lives since long ago, that trees which resembled *sugi* but weren't actually *sugi* would, one after the other, be named *sugi*. . . . and so it goes with this tree.

Real *sugi* were, originally, either of the Taxodiaceae family or the Cupressaceae family.

It is thanks to the study of molecular phylogenetics, which has blossomed since the 1990s, that this is already so ambiguous. This is the case with the APG categorization system for angiosperms as well—DNA doesn't clear things up. I need to try to accept the fact that the Taxodiaceae family has been incorporated into the Cupressaceae family, in the same way that I accepted the gradual dissolution of the Liliaceae family. But long ago, when the Taxodiaceae family was just the Taxodiaceae family plain and simple—a state of affairs I found calming—it included several types of *sugi*, like the Japanese *sugi*, but also the sequoias.

I have talked many times about being moved emotionally by the giant trees in Sequoia National Park. I have also talked about being moved by the giant trees while passing through Redwood National Park.

North America is a continent of amazing rock formations. Rocks that have been living through time on a global scale—the Grand Canyon, Monument Valley, the canyon of Zion National Park, Bryce Canyon—they close in on you here with their amazing colors and scale. But the sequoias, which have lived up to several thousand years of age—their presence eclipses these rocks.

When I stood in front of the giant tree named "Sherman" in Sequoia National Park, as I faced this lifeform that was so much larger than I was and had long surpassed me in age, I thought my feelings at the time must be similar to that of having a religious faith or belief. I am certain that I would not feel the same way facing a person, no matter who it was, nor facing an elephant, no matter how large it was, nor even when facing a tiger with an empty stomach at the moment I was to be eaten.

At the time, I wasn't quite fifty years old; I was tiny, helpless, just a speck. My companion was a giant tree, two thousand and several hundred years old, and yet still reproducing, continuing to add young trees to the surrounding area. I wondered if I'd be swallowed by this lifeforce—but it wasn't the same as with a tiger. It wasn't as if I was going to be destroyed, eaten, or even hurt. More so than "being swallowed," I had the sense it was more like a "being received," just as one is.

There is a saying that "all living things possess Buddha nature." It seems there have been many debates about whether this is true for inanimate things such as mountains, rivers, grasses, and trees. I don't know what conclusion they have reached. However, no matter how long I stare in wonder at the rocks and valleys of the Grand Canyon or Monument Valley, that saying never comes to mind. But every time I see a giant sequoia, I think: "There's no way that doesn't possess Buddha nature."

Those sequoias are ex-Taxodiaceae. Included in the ex-Taxodiaceae family are just a few genera, one of which is the type of giant tree found in Sequoia National Park, like the one named "Sherman," or the one named "Grant," which bears the name of an old army general and boasts the largest size of all of them. If you call them by their scientific name, they are *Sequoiadendron giganteum*, of the genus *Sequoiadendron* and the ex-Taxodiaceae family.

Now they say the giant trees of Redwood National Park are among the world's tallest, and those too are ex-Taxodiaceae: they are called *Sequoia sempervirens* of the genus *Sequoia*.

And as for the Japanese *sugi*, they are called *Cryptomeria japonica*, of the ex-Taxodiaceae (or *sugi*) family and of the genus *Cryptomeria* (also *sugi*).

The *sugi* which have grown native in Japan since time immemorial, those *sugi* that started out as tiny grasses—it made me happy that those *sugi* were close relatives of these giant trees (there is a saying that goes: "Protection comes in the shadow of large trees"). And now that the Taxodiaceae family has been incorporated into the Cupressaceae family and the sequoias and the *sugi* have been separated, I have become absolutely and completely devastated.

To go to Takachiho from Kumamoto, you have to pass the town of Takamori in Minami Aso, and then head east. There is an old *sugi* in Takamori. It is a tree called the Takamoridono no sugi. They say that in this spot, four hundred years ago, in the Tenshō era, a powerful local clan named Takamori lost a battle and the feudal lord committed *seppuku*, slicing open his belly. I don't know whether the *sugi* grew as a memorial to this act of *seppuku*, or if the tree was already there and he committed *seppuku* while leaning against it, but in any case, it is a spot soaked with blood.

When I went there for the first time, I was shocked. You see, on the side of the road in Takamori there stands, inconspicuously, a small sign that seems meant to be overlooked. Without overlooking it, I turned and zig-zagged along the narrow path. And then there was a small gate on the path, which was, quite rudely, shut. A lock was wrapped around it and so it appeared as if it couldn't be opened or closed. For the faint of heart, this was the end of the line. But when I looked closer, there was a note hanging from the gate. It read: "Many people have come here to see the tree as of late because of a TV program. Hunters, please be careful." Across the way was a pasture, and there were several cows looking this way suspiciously. Inside the gate was also a pasture, and so cows roamed around on the inside. It seemed the lock was meant to keep the cows from running away. While the cows remained suspicious, I undid the lock and went inside, then closed the gate and returned the lock back to the way it was. Inside, it was hard to tell if there was a path or not. There's a sudden rise in elevation. I'm out of breath. Flowers are in bloom, either of the Liliaceae family, the Asteraceae family, or the Apiaceae family. There's cow dung all over. Seems like I'll end up stepping in some. The path-that-may-or-may-not-be-a-path continues forward toward a grove of *sugi*. It is luxuriant. There is a sign small enough for an ant that points into the grove of trees, and so I have no choice but to bend over and descend into the cavity-like center of the grove. What overwhelmed me as I came into the middle of it was the feeling of vibrant motion that I sensed from the *sugi* (there were two of them). I did not get this sense of vibrant motion from any of the large *sugi* elsewhere. The branches of these *sugi* twisted and turned, and before my eyes they split in two. One went up and the other went left and right—it looked as if they were leaping up and down. Before my eyes they reached the heavens, and then came back down to earth, wrapping up the space in between and creating what looked like a giant dome with an arched ceiling. Branches and leaves grew thickly out from their trunks. Tree sap circulated from tip to tip. Words that I knew from the Lotus Sutra came pouring out of my mouth: "Big roots, big stems, big branches, and big leaves." Surrounding the *sugi* trees were groves of glossy-leaved evergreens. With the sunlight filtering through them, each leaf shone brilliantly, one by one. I wanted to chant more from the *Lotus Sutra*: "Medium roots, medium stems, medium branches, and medium leaves." And then small vines, small mosses, and small ferns covered over everything, they covered over the bark of the tree trunks, they covered over the skin of the earth. Once again, I desire to continue chanting: "Small roots, small stems, small branches, and small leaves."

"Little ones to him belong / they are weak but he is strong"—this I also want to chant (although it is from an old, old translation of a certain hymn from the Meiji era). It continues: "Yes, Jesus loves me / Yes, Jesus loves me / For the Bible tells me so."

The fact that one is able to confirm one's smallness and weakness when something bigger and stronger stands in front of it, and that it's ok to be small and weak, and that if you rely on this something big, that you can then go on living your life as yourself, just as you are—the many ways of expressing these ideas were packed tightly into the space around me, and they made me feel warm inside.

TRAVELING WITH SEITAKA-AWADACHISŌ

On top of my desk sits some thoroughly dried out and crumbling *seitaka-awadachisō*. The fresh yellow color it had when I picked it has faded away. It's something I brought home with me from Michigan.

I went to that city in Michigan that starts with the letter "K" in the beginning of September, and I saw *seitaka-awadachisō* growing there. It was native *seitaka-awadachisō*, growing in its native habitat—the kind that I was unable to find in California.

I changed planes in Chicago. I got off the plane, and the moment I stepped onto the jet bridge leading to the gate, a hot, humid gust of wind came blowing in through the gaps. I had heard from many Midwesterners that the Midwestern summer was hot and humid, and they were right. Unbelievably hot, with a humidity I did not expect. The weather report had it around thirty degrees Celsius, which is nothing compared to the summer in Japan. In Japan it gets to thirty-five or thirty-six on average, but the heat here gets amplified because it's inland, as does the cold, and it gets extremely harsh. I met eyes with an airport employee and smiled, saying, "It's hot, huh?" They replied, "Last week was worse. It's only going to get hotter." From there I boarded a small plane and headed to K. airport. It was hot there, too, and humid. The friend who picked me up at the airport was wearing the kind of light clothing people wore in California. (Standard dress in California is a T-shirt and shorts. A T-shirt and jeans is considered formal attire.)

On the way back from the airport, I saw yellow flowers blooming here and there.

We passed by several clusters of these flowers, and I finally realized that they were *seitaka-awadachisō*. They were short, so I wasn't convinced that I was correct. They were, at most, one meter in height. I had thought that here, where they were native and grow free, they must grow taller than they do in Japan. I had figured that they would cover over the fields in full flourish, spreading their seeds as they swayed in the wind, billowing in waves to the point of overtaking the whole field.

"I found it," I told my friend in English, "'Goldenrod' (which is the English name for *seitaka-awadachisō*), it was blooming along the road, in vacant lots." I explained: "I have always wanted to see it, that was one of the reasons I came to this country."

My friend replied in Japanese, saying: "There's *seitaka-awadachisō* everywhere." This friend and I usually spoke to each other in Japanese. It just so happened that there was someone with us who did not understand Japanese, so that's why I used English.

There was a forest behind my friend's house. The house had a giant window facing the forest. You could look out at the trees of the forest as if you were on a safari, looking at animals from a car surrounded in glass. I saw all kinds of animals that cut through the forest. Squirrels climbed up and down the trees. Chipmunks gnawed at the food that was left outside for them. They would hear a sound and then run off into the bushes. A little while after I started watching, several deer showed up. They passed by without making a sound, stretching out their necks and pulling them back in. And then a little later some turkeys appeared. First a group of females passed by, and then a group consisting only of males passed by.

I asked my friend the names of the trees in the forest, and he said that there were several oaks. I knew oaks from the Japanese dessert called *kashiwa-mochi*, which are wrapped in oak leaves. In Japanese we make a distinction: if it's a deciduous oak, we call it a *nara*, but if it's an evergreen, we call it a *kashi*. So what was growing in the forest here were *nara*, among other trees.

My friend said: "You can't see it now, but in winter, when the leaves fall, you can see the house across the way clearly."

On the ground stood dried-up stems with red seeds. I said that they were called *mamushigusa* in Japanese, and my friend told me they were called "jack-in-the-pulpit" in English and explained what that meant to me in Japanese. The *gibōshi* (or plantain lilies) that had been so carefully planted around the edges of the house had been completely destroyed by deer (which had munched on them), and it appeared that they would no longer be able to bloom.

"That's poison ivy," my friend said, pointing at a vine underfoot. "It's a member of the Anacardiaceae family, and if you touch it, you'll get a terrible rash. I thought I might pull it up and burn it, but even just inhaling the smoke is poisonous. It's truly an impossible plant to deal with."

While it was still light outside, we went with a few people to go eat dinner. There's a local beer here called Oberon, and it's refreshing, with a delicate, citrus-like aroma. It's really delicious. I wanted to order some, but everyone told me it was the wrong season. This city that starts with the letter K is full of breweries. Naturally, the people who live here love beer, and everyone, including my friend, and my friend's friends, and their friends' friends—everyone knows a lot about beer. According to them, Oberon is a wheat beer, and you make wheat beers in the summer, but since it was now autumn, there were no wheat beers available. It was so hot, and it was still September—how was it "autumn"? I couldn't comprehend this at all.

On the following day, the temperature rose to thirty-five degrees. People said it was the hottest this summer had been. Young men walked around with no shirts on. Young women walked around showing off their upper and lower bodies.

On the third day it was thirty-three degrees, and it wasn't humid. And then that evening it rained. It was a real rain, the kind that never falls on Southern California. It felt fresh. It stopped falling after a few hours. In the middle of the night, I stood on the street fresh with rain and looked up at the sky. The crescent moon appeared and disappeared in the spaces between passing clouds.

On the fourth day the temperature dropped a few degrees. On the oak trees, acorns that were the same color as its green leaves had grown in dense clusters. Fruit was growing on the apple trees as well. The apples were just starting to change color. On the shoulder of the highway, thickets of sumac that were similar in color to the green Chinese sumac caught my eye. They had red seeds attached to them. There were some that had leaves that were turning red. And then, naturally, the *seitaka-awadachisō* was yellow.

When was it that I first started caring about *seitaka-awadachisō*? In middle school, I liked the change in the seasons, and anytime the newspaper would carry an article about the change in weather or plants, I would cut it out and paste it into a scrapbook. And then my father bought me a *saijiki*—a collection of seasonal words and phrases that are used in classical Japanese poetry. It was the *New Haiku Saijiki* by Yamamoto Kenkichi and it was divided into five volumes: Spring, Summer, Autumn, Winter, and New Year's. I lapped it up. What I read with great enthusiasm weren't the example poems, but rather the explanations of the seasonal words and phrases. I liked the ones for late summer and autumn. I was convinced that my interest in *seitaka-awadachisō* came from its description in this *saijiki* collection, but now, as I leaf through my old worn-out copy over and over again, I cannot find "*seitaka-awadachisō*," nor any variation thereof.

Instead, I found a page on *arechinogiku*, which was where it had always been. I remembered being moved by the description that was written there: "The name *arechinogiku* means wasteland (*arechi*) chrysanthemum (*kiku*) if we take the word '*no*' as a possessive, but if we understand the '*no*' as the word that means 'wild,' then it feels like a wasteland (*arechi*) wild chrysanthemum (*nogiku*)."That is how I tried to live in that period of my life, embracing those words and "feeling like a wasteland wild chrysanthemum."

After I entered university, I read the *Butsurui shōko*, a dictionary of the Edo dialect (Edo being the old name for Tokyo) compiled by poet Koshigaya Gozan in 1775. This is it, I thought to myself, this is the world I had wanted to know about. It was a world of words that changed with the seasons. Wind, stars, and plants all changed with the seasons, and their names changed depending on their location. There was nothing constant. Each thing got a name, and received power from those words, and lived vividly, and underwent change.

Before long, I began writing poetry. I read somewhere (probably in a *saijiki*, but I don't know whose version) that another name for *seitaka-awadachisō* was *akinokirinsō*. This shook me to my core, and I wrote the following poem:

> *Akikirinsō* crowds together
> And now
> Bright, bright yellow
> It's really *seitaka-awadachisō*

Ah. . . . how young I was. I feel embarrassed as I copy it down now. But at that time, as I would repeat over and over, "*seitaka-awadachisō, ō-arechinogiku,*" I had the feeling that I was putting into words the things I kept pent up in my heart. I was putting into words the impatience I felt, along with the anxieties I felt about my very existence that I could do nothing about.

A little while later, someone pointed out to me that *seitaka-awadachisō* and *akinokirinsō* were different plants. I looked it up and it was true. *Seitaka-awadachisō* belonged to the Asteraceae family, and was a part of the genus *Solidago*, the word for which is *akinoki-*

rinsō in Japanese. Then there's another plant actually called *akinoki-rinsō* in the *Solidago* or *akinokirinsō* genus. *Seitaka-awadachisō* is a naturalized species, whereas *akinokirinsō* is native. In fall, they both bloom yellow flowers in clusters along the roadside.

I was embarrassed to have written that poem without knowing this truth, but I left the poem as it was. At the time, I wasn't yet the plant-fanatic that I am now, so it didn't worry me too much. Now that I've looked it up and can clearly tell the difference between the two, I get the sense that the difference between them is like that between white bean-paste and black bean-paste—everyone calls both of them "bean-paste." Even in the field guide I bought a few years ago called *Rural Plants of Southern Kyushu*—that one I walk around with, never letting it out of my hands—it says on the page for *seitaka-awadachisō* that another name for the plant is *"seitaka-akinokirinsō,"* and on the page for *akinokirinsō*, it says that another name for this plant is *"seitaka-awadachisō."*

That's how it goes, in the end, with names. There is nothing that's truly absolute.

On the fifth day, the day I was to return home from Michigan, it cooled down even more. It was a coolness that gave one confidence that those hot days would not come back. It was like everything was running downhill all at once. On the road to the airport, I noticed so many more *seitaka-awadachisō* plants than I had seen a few days before. Each and every one was a vibrant yellow.

I got my friend to stop the car, and I walked up to the *seita-ka-awadachisō* that was growing wild on the side of the road. I touched it. And then I cut off the top part, where the cluster of flowers bloomed. I put it into a Ziplock bag (the fact that I always had one on me was proof that I was a drifter who moved around via plane) and hid it within the depths of my luggage. Transporting plants across state lines is a clear violation of the law. Because there are people who do this kind of thing, plants continue to immigrate.

When I boarded the plane at K. Airport, a cold wind came blowing in through the gaps of the jet bridge.

From the plane, I could see Lake Michigan down below. It spread out without boundaries, and I couldn't see the opposite shoreline. I thought there must not be an opposite shore. A few years before this, I had stood on the bank of Lake Michigan. At that time, too, I couldn't see the opposite shoreline, and I thought there must not be one. The water was clear. The waves rolled in, and then back out. Many small shells had washed up on the sandy shoreline. It was like the lake were an ocean. Except that here, there was a stillness that felt like sterilization, like the exact opposite of fertility.

What I am faced with each day is the Pacific Ocean of Southern California. There are long sandy beaches that stretch on and on. There are waves that roll in and then roll back out. There is a horizon line in which the sun sets. The beach, the sea, the waves— they're all grandiose, and noisy, and smelly. It's a pervasive smell that cannot be captured by words like "fragrance" or "stink." The water is flavored by salt and seaweed, and the minute you touch it, it feels like it could wrap you up and take you off somewhere. As we beings that live and die, we sentient beings, as we laugh boisterously, it readies to take us away. It's that kind of sea, the Pacific Ocean.

As we crossed over this large, wide, freshwater sea that was Lake Michigan, I stared at the *seitaka-awadachisō* that I had successfully snuck onto the plane. And I thought to myself, "Just what was it that I had witnessed on this trip?" I had the feeling that I had borne witness to something important. Something very important.

I thought about it for a while, and then I realized: "Seasons." I happened to be there right as summer ended and autumn began, and I realized that I had observed that exact moment with my very eyes.

FLORA, FAUNA, AFTERWORD

Over the twenty-one or so months that these chapters were serialized in publisher Iwanami Shoten's periodical *Tosho*, all I thought about were plants. When I stepped outdoors, plants were the only thing that I noticed. I forced my way into the world of the internet to search for plants, and somehow, I haven't been able to find my way back to reality. I had a strong feeling that I might actually be made of grass. More grass than human. Or that maybe I was a tree. Or a vine. For some twenty-one-or-so months, I lived with that feeling. You could even say that I was entangled in this feeling.

During the same period of time, I was publishing serialized articles in the periodical *Bungakkai* about dogs—about dogs growing old. Those articles became the book *The Heart of a Dog* (or *Inugokoro* in Japanese). In the end, "heart" is the same thing as "spirit."

That book was about fauna. This book is about flora. In both, I was supposed to chronicle how fauna and flora live, but death came floating up from the depths. Or rather, when focused on "death," I saw "life" come trailing behind.

For some twenty-one months, I thought intently about the life and death of plants. I thought that I had captured in writing everything I wanted to say for the time being about the plants in my immediate vicinity, and so I stopped writing these articles for *Tosho*. It was the end of September.

Right after that, I visited a mountain village called Shiramine in Ishikawa Prefecture.

The mountain roads there were teeming with plant life. There was no end to them. I had finished nothing, I had captured nothing in writing. One after another, I met plants that I had been longing to meet. I had known them from guidebooks and from my *saijiki*, but this was my first time seeing the real things, and I almost felt like bowing before them, one by one, and formally greeting them: "Ah, I have heard so much about you . . ." I met *akinokirinsō*, or *Solidago virgaurea*. I met *akinonogeshi*, or *Lactuca indica*. I met *kawara-yomogi*, or *Artemisia capillaris*. I met *nurude*, or *Rhus javanica*. Each of them had on their autumn face. I even met *akebi*, or *Akebia quinata*. It had its mouth wide open. I was happy and excited as I plucked off the fruit from the vine. I plucked the inside of the fruit out with my fingers and ate it. It was sticky and sweet.

Autumn in these mountains was full of noisy sounds. It was brimming with signs of life that were repeating the cycle of birth and death, similar to what I've experienced while walking along the coast of the Pacific Ocean.

In the beginning of November, I went to Berlin.

It was the dark period before Christmas. I went the previous year at the same time, and everything was covered in white snow. This time, though, no snow fell whatsoever. It was cloudy, dark, and cold every day. What caught my eye as I walked around in this weather were the Christmas ornaments hanging in the windows of the houses I passed. Although they were the same kind of electric bulbs, these decorations were completely different from the garish ones you find in the US. For the most part, these decorations could be described as "lights" or "stars." Which is to say, they expressed a meaning, a hope. The already short period of daily sunlight was getting even shorter and shorter. The sky was cloudy and dark. I got a real sense that what everyone was eagerly waiting for amidst all of this was not a birthday celebration, but rather a chance to take the light back into their own hands.

Mistletoe had gathered among the bare trees. It sat plump and vigorous on the branches, to the extent that I wondered whether it might break them. Mistletoe is used as a Christmas decoration, so you find it for sale here and there. The mistletoe I saw nearby had verdant leaves and transparent, round berries that had soaked up the sunlight and were shining brilliantly.

There's a drought now in California.

There's one every year, but this year is really bad. People say it's the worst it's been in twenty years. I came to California about twenty years ago. There was a drought then too, and people said that it had been several years since there was any rain. California has a drought and a water shortage every year (excluding 1998, when there was El Niño or La Niña or whichever it was that brought heavy rains for the first time in a hundred years), but this is the first time I've seen it as bad as it is this year.

Sage stands dried and withered in the wasteland. Its leaves are just as they were last year, its branches are dry and break off with a cracking sound. Every branch, every stem, remain without a single flower. Surely the drought gets worse every year. If it keeps on going like this, year after year, for hundreds of years, the plants of this place will completely dry up. And then they'll probably have to change their forms to survive. Lamiaceae, Onagraceae, Gentiana-ceae—each of these will lose their leaves and grow thorns. They'll become like family to cacti and agave, and they'll cover the ground. I can vividly imagine this state of affairs.

Plants changing from one state of being into another. Not dying, not perishing.

That's right, plants don't die.

I had thought that only dogs and humans lived a single life and then died.

But I was wrong. I, myself, am a human, and I've spent my life with dogs and other humans, and I have become accustomed to them. And because I make a distinction between each individual dog and human, I imagine that if I were a plant—a *kyūrigusa* or something like it, or sage or geranium or *ōinu-no-fuguri* or *karasu-no-endō*—that I would make a distinction between each and every plant. From this micro viewpoint, I, myself, and a *kyūrigusa* as well, are nothing more than beings that live and then die. Or perhaps we are nothing more than beings that do not die, do not perish. I, myself, and *kyūrigusa* as well—we are, just as we are, the enormous power of the cosmos.

I witnessed the death of my father and the death of my dog, and I watched the process closely. They were like trees and grass as they withered away, my father and dog who died slowly. And both my father and my dog breathed rapid, painful breaths. For a long period of time, I watched closely as my both my father and my dog grew old. But all the same, even as I thought, "They'll die someday, but they'll live until then," by no means did I think, "Now is the moment that they will die." The painful breaths subsided. And then the breathing became peaceful. It was like they weren't confronting anything anymore, my father and my dog both. They breathed peacefully, as if they were merely walking down a calm, level path in front of them. One breath. Two breaths. The third breath never came. That was where the breathing stopped. That was death.

As if nimbly stepping over a line on the ground, they crossed over to the other side.

That was a human's death, that was a dog's death.

They will not come back to this side.

Dogs and humans both, if seen from a macro viewpoint, are nothing more than a speck in a larger flow, repeating a cycle of birth and death on top of this blue planet. Not even a speck. Something even smaller. More transient. The death and rebirth of a plant, and this death for which there is no rebirth—just how different are they?

I am grateful to many people, in many places, with whom I have come into contact through plants. Ultimately, I thought I should focus only on the plants in this book, and so I made all these people anonymous by referring to them as "my friend." These include Irmela Hijiya-Kirschnereit and Hijiya Shūji of Berlin, Reiko Abe of Oslo, Jeffrey Angles of Michigan, Nakazawa Kei of Tokyo, Baba Junji of Kumamoto, and Stewart Johnson, also of Kumamoto.

And I am grateful for Kikuchi Nobuyoshi, who designed the book. And Becky Cohen for her photographs. And also Tokuda Takeko of Iwanami Shoten's *Tosho*. And Higuchi Yoshizumi of the Editing Department.

The faces and voices of these people float to mind, and I am filled with gratitude as I write down their names. I can't help but feel uneasy about the fact that I cannot give each of them their own scientific name.

HIROMI ITO

March 2014

NOTES

1. Bashō, Matsuo. *Bashō's Journey: The Literary Prose of Matsuo Bashō.* Trans. David Landis Barnhill. Albany: State University of New York Press, 2005. p. 62.
2. Keene, Donald. *Dawn to the West.* New York: Columbia University Press, 1999. p. 311.
3. Murasaki Shikibu. *The Tale of Genji.* Trans. Royall Tyler. New York: Penguin Books, 2003. p. 55.
4 Itō, Hiromi. *Wild Grass on the Riverbank.* Trans. Jeffrey Angles. Notre Dame: Action Books, 2015. p. 52.
5 *Kojiki.* Trans. Donald Philippi. Princeton: Princeton University Press, 1969. p. 89.

ACKNOWLEDGEMENTS

I would first like to thank Hiromi Ito for writing this book and trusting me with its translation. I have learned so much from Ito's writing, and it is a true honor to share space on this book's cover with her. I would also like to thank Jeffrey Angles for putting me in touch with Ito, and for his blessing in taking this project on. I would like to thank everyone at Nightboat Books for their support with and enthusiasm for this translation. In particular, I would like to thank Trisha Low, Lindsey Boldt, Stephen Motika, and Gia Gonzales. I thank *Asymptote* journal for publishing an early version of the chapter "Living Trees and Dying Trees" from this collection, and for interviewing both Ito and me in conjunction with its publication.

I am indebted to my colleagues/friends Margherita Long, Pedro Bassoe, and Daryl Maude for their encouragement and help along the way. I am forever in debt to Sakae Fujita-sensei of the University of California, Santa Cruz. I would like to express my gratitude to Reiko Abe Auestad for arranging a reading from this manuscript in Oslo, and for helping me better understand Ito's work. I am grateful to my graduate and undergraduate students at the University of California, Irvine who have read various iterations of this translation. Their comments and suggestions were encouraging and insightful.

Special thanks to Katherine Aungier for recommending Night-boat Books as a potential publisher. And special thanks to my mother, Jacqueline Carroll, for helping me see the importance of plants from an early age. This translation would not have happened without the love and support of Petronella Keryn Sovella, my partner in gardening and in life. And in the spirit of this book about tree spirits and grass spirits, I would like to thank the following plants for helping me understand the meaning of this book: the papaya tree and passionfruit vines on my veranda, the clumps of sage and cacti living in the UC Irvine Ecological Preserve, and the eucalyptus trees soon to be removed from the UC Irvine campus.

HIROMI ITO is an award-winning Japanese poet. She is well-known for her unconventional style and engagement with issues of gender and immigration, as well as for her deep attention to plant life. Much of Ito's writing since the 1990s has explored her time living in Southern California in the United States. Her 1998 novella *House Plant* was nominated for the Akutagawa Prize for Literature. Ito translated *House Plant* into English with the help of her late husband Harold Cohen, and it was published in *U.S.—Japan Women's Journal* in 2007. Two books of her poetry have also been translated into English: *Wild Grass on the Riverbank* and *Killing Kanoko: Selected Poems of Hiromi Itō* (both translated by Jeffrey Angles and published by Action Books). Angles' translation of her novel *The Thorn Puller* was published by Stone Bridge Press in 2022.

JON L PITT is an educator, translator, and musician. He received his PhD from the University of California, Berkeley and is Assistant Professor of East Asian Studies at the University of California, Irvine. His current book project is titled *Becoming Botanical: Rethinking the Human through Plant Life in Modern Japan*. He is the host of the podcast *Nature : Mono*.

NIGHTBOAT BOOKS

Nightboat Books, a nonprofit organization, seeks to develop audiences for writers whose work resists convention and transcends boundaries. We publish books rich with poignancy, intelligence, and risk. Please visit nightboat.org to learn about our titles and how you can support our future publications.

The following individuals have supported the publication of this book. We thank them for their generosity and commitment to the mission of Nightboat Books:

Kazim Ali
Anonymous (4)
Abraham Avnisan
Jean C. Ballantyne
The Robert C. Brooks Revocable Trust
Amanda Greenberger
Rachel Lithgow
Anne Marie Macari
Elizabeth Madans
Elizabeth Motika
Thomas Shardlow
Benjamin Taylor
Jerrie Whitfield & Richard Motika

This book is made possible, in part, by grants from the New York City Department of Cultural Affairs in partnership with the City Council, the New York State Council on the Arts Literature Program, and the Topanga Fund, which is dedicated to promoting the arts and literature of California.

NYC Cultural Affairs   NEW YORK STATE OF OPPORTUNITY. Council on the Arts